# GOAL REDEEMER

# GOAL REDEEMER

*10 Principles for Overcoming Barriers to Achieving Your Goals and Fulfilling Your God-Given Dreams*

KEMI AKINTEWE, PhD

Institute for New Victory, LLC
Orlando, Florida

Copyright © 2023 by Kemi Akintewe

All rights reserved. This book or any portion thereof may not be reproduced or used in any manner whatsoever without the express written permission of the publisher except for the use of brief quotations in a book review.

Published and distributed in the United States
by Institute for New Victory, LLC.
1317 Edgewater Drive, Suite 5364
Orlando, FL 32804

Hardcover ISBN: 979-8-9874126-2-6
Paperback ISBN: 979-8-9874126-3-3
eBook ISBN: 979-8-9874126-4-0
Library of Congress Control Number: 2022922754

First Edition, March 2023

Printed in the United States of America.

The author of this book does not dispense medical advice or prescribe the use of any technique as a form of treatment for physical, emotional, or medical problems without the advice of a physician, either directly or indirectly. The intent of the author is only to offer information of a general nature to help you in your quest for emotional and spiritual well-being. In the event you use any of the information in this book for yourself, which is your constitutional right, the author and the publisher assume no responsibility for your actions.

All Scripture quotations, unless otherwise indicated, are taken from the Holy Bible, New International Version®, NIV®. Copyright ©1973, 1978, 1984, 2011 by Biblica, Inc.™ Used by permission of Zondervan. All rights reserved worldwide.

Scripture quotations marked AMP are taken from the Amplified® Bible (AMP), copyright © 2015 by The Lockman Foundation. Used by permission. www.lockman.org

Scripture quotations marked ESV are from the ESV® Bible (The Holy Bible, English Standard Version®), copyright © 2001 by Crossway Bibles, a publishing ministry of Good News Publishers. Used by permission. All rights reserved.

Scripture quotations marked KJV are taken from the King James Version Bible.

Scripture quotations marked NKJV are taken from the New King James Version of the Bible. Copyright © 1982 by Thomas Nelson, Inc. Used by permission. All rights reserved.

Scripture quotations marked CSB®, are taken from the Christian Standard Bible®, Copyright © 2017 by Holman Bible Publishers. Used by permission. Christian Standard Bible®, and CSB® are federally registered trademarks of Holman Bible Publishers.

Scripture quotations marked NLT are taken from the Holy Bible, New Living Translation, copyright © 1996, 2004, 2015 by Tyndale House Foundation. All rights reserved. Used by permission of Tyndale House Publishers, Carol Stream, Illinois 60188.

Scripture quotations marked CEV are from the Contemporary English Version Copyright © 1991, 1992, 1995 by American Bible Society, Used by Permission.

Scripture quotations marked GNT are from the Good News Translation in Today's English Version- Second Edition Copyright © 1992 by American Bible Society. Used by Permission.

Scripture quotations marked MSG or "The Message" are taken from The Message. Copyright © 1993, 1994, 1995, 1996, 2000, 2001, 2002. Used by permission of NavPress Publishing Group.

PRAISE FOR
# *GOAL REDEEMER*

"Insightful and encouraging! The *Goal Redeemer* book is a must-read for everyone aspiring to live life to the fullest and fulfill their dreams."

Mercy Adebayo
Author of *Something About Grace,*
*It Doesn't Have to End There: A Walk with Peter,*
and *Hope While You Wait*

"I have witnessed the transformational impact Dr. Kemi's coaching techniques have had on the lives of women, and I am beyond excited to see those techniques now captured in this book! Dr. Kemi and I are "goal-sisters" and have worked hand-in-hand to facilitate the *Women Empowerment and Building (W.E.B) ministry*. During this time, I've watched Dr. Kemi grow as an influencer with women in the community and professionally as a biomedical engineering Professor. I know God has ordained this next chapter in her life as an author, and I promise this book's words of wisdom will inspire you to pursue and maximize your God-given potential."

Nancy Lewis
Financial Literacy Coach

"The *Goal Redeemer* book is a perfect blend of Scripture, practical applications, and rich storytelling. These words have soul assignments, and I feel blessed to have been chosen to contribute."

Ellena Balkcom
Founder, Written on Purpose Communications, LLC

"For those struggling to set goals and realize their dreams, look no further. Dr. Kemi lays a clear foundation of Godly wisdom and kingdom principles that will help you along your journey. This book is designed to position you for greatness and help you accomplish the goals God has already placed inside you. The three key frameworks that she shares are spot on! They are thought-provoking and provide powerful insights needed to know yourself, overcome internal and external interference, and act intentionally to achieve your goals. Her authenticity and transparency are relatable and captivating! Dr. Kemi using her personal journey of struggle and triumph on her road to healing, setting goals, and realizing her dreams, provides the reader with hope and aspiration to know they are not alone on their journey. It also shows the reader that their goals, dreams, and aspirations do not have to be limited to their culture, environment, or past negative experiences. By the time you finish doing the work provided in *Goal Redeemer*, not only will you envision your dreams, but you will be well on your way to achieving your goals! With God, all things are possible."

Sandra Heard
CEO, Heard Empowerment LLC
Life Coach | Educator | Speaker
Author of *The Power of Forgiveness The Road To Healing and Restoration*
Co-Author of *POWER MOMs 3.0 Stories of Triumph Through The Lenses of Powerful Women of Faith*

For my loving husband, Tunde,
my relentless cheerleader and
father to our beautiful children, Toye and Teni.
Thank you for your love, support, and
encouragement to start writing.

"But now, GOD's Message,
the God who made you in the first place, Jacob,
the One who got you started, Israel:
'Don't be afraid,' **I've redeemed you**.
I've called your name. You're mine.
When you're in over your head, I'll be there with you.
When you're in rough waters, you will not go down.
When you're between a rock and a hard place,
it won't be a dead end—
Because I am GOD, your personal God,
The Holy of Israel, your Savior.
I paid a huge price for you:
all of Egypt, with rich Cush and Seba thrown in!
*That's* how much you mean to me!
*That's* how much I love you!
I'd sell off the whole world to get you back,
trade the creation just for you.
'Forget about what's happened;
don't keep going over old history.
Be alert, be present. I'm about to do something brand-new.
It's bursting out! Don't you see it?
There it is! I'm making a road through the desert,
rivers in the badlands.'"
(Isaiah 43:1-4, 18-19 MSG)

# CONTENTS

Foreword ............................................................................. 1
Preface ................................................................................ 3

**PART I    Know Thyself**
Chapter 1 – Practice Self-Reflection ................................................ 9
Chapter 2 – Perform Self-Assessments ......................................... 23

**PART II    Conquer Your Internal and External Interference**
Chapter 3 – Principle 1 Believe in Your Goals ............................. 37
Chapter 4 – Principle 2 Overcome Discouragement ................... 47
Chapter 5 – Principle 3 Forgive Yourself and Others .................. 59
Chapter 6 – Principle 4 Overcome Your Fears and Walk in Boldness ...... 71
Chapter 7 – Principle 5 Develop Patience and Perseverance ...... 97
Chapter 8 – Principle 6 Have Authority Over Your Thoughts ................ 111

**PART III    Act Intentionally Toward Achieving Your Goals**
Chapter 9 – Principle 7 Manage Your Time and Avoid Procrastination 133
Chapter 10 – Principle 8 Be Self-Motivated ................................ 151
Chapter 11 – Principle 9 Engage in Conscientious Relationships ........... 161
Chapter 12 – Principle 10 Communicate Your Goals ................ 171

Acknowledgments ..................................................................... 181
About the Author ....................................................................... 183
Bibliography ............................................................................... 185

# Foreword

In a world where everything is moving at a warped speed, words like goals, discipline, and commitment seem to fade because of the desire to achieve everything now. Dr. Kemi Akintewe's book, **Goal Redeemer: 10 Principles for Overcoming Barriers to Achieving your Goals and Fulfilling Your God-given Dreams**, could not have graced us at a better time. I started reading this book with the intention of giving a review, but as I dived in, this book inspired me to go back and look at my own life to redeem my goals. So often, we put off our goals because we think too much time has passed, or we fear we will fail because we don't have the skill set to accomplish them. But the hope this book brings is refreshing and empowering! The times ahead will demand a set of people willing to commit to long- term goals and persevere no matter what challenges may arise. A set of people hungry for something more than glitz and glamour, people who are longing to see the Kingdom come to earth. I also believe God will continue to raise Kingdom leaders like Dr. Akintewe to equip this remnant. She takes you on a journey of practicality, yet the pages are infused with the power of God's Word, which breathes faith into the dry places of lost dreams. Dr. Akintewe describes the steps needed to accomplish the God-given dreams placed within your soul from inception. She not only gives you academic tools to achieve your goals, but her life experiences prove the Goal Redeemer lives and is available today to help you accomplish His will for your life.

If you feel despondent, trapped by your past mistakes, inadequate, rejected, or hopeless about your goals, I encourage you to take hold of the principles written within and give your dreams a chance to live again. The past is gone, yet it is a major stronghold and hindrance to achieving your goals, and Dr. Akintewe gives you the steps to free yourself from the prison of the past. This may be the appointed time for what you were anointed for many years ago to come to fruition finally. This book will be a potent tool for anyone from any walk of life who desires to fulfill their God-purpose. I encourage you to allow the Holy Spirit to work through the precept-upon-precept style of this book to build on the already solid foundation of Jesus Christ.

As you embark on this journey of redeeming your goals, I pray for the blessing and gift of Dr. Akintewe's life to touch you in some small way. I pray her wisdom and intelligence, vulnerability and transparency, love for serving humanity, and willingness and obedience to her God will not only inspire you but also empower you to go after your God-given dreams. May this book unlock your hidden potential and allow you to see that nothing is impossible with the Goal-Redeemer!

Lisa Singh
Author, Pastor
Heavenly Grace Ministries
Queens, New York

Books Authored:
*Created on Purpose for Purpose*
*Words. They Become You!*
*The Scandal of Identity Theft: Reclaim Your Identity*
*Issues of the Heart Devotional*

## Preface

Your best life is right before you. As you read this book, learn from your past, position yourself to grow, and prepare to encounter divine direction. Now is your season for the manifestation of your dreams, your appointed time to accomplish those goals buried inside you. I started writing this book with the end in mind. Most of my early speaking engagements started with vision planning and goal-setting workshops for women in local communities. This book reveals how to plan successfully, identify your core distractions (interferences), and create spaces to remove barriers that prevent you from achieving your God-given goals. Believe that God single-handedly inspired your goals that align with His Word. Now is your time to give birth to them.

As you journey through this book, I share my experiences, beliefs and understanding of God's model for reaching our full potential using three frameworks to live out our destinies. The first framework is to *Know Thyself*. Before any work can be done in one's life, the knowledge of who you are brings awareness to what you truly want. A self-reflection and assessment let you dig deeper into your life and help to identify what you need to develop to reach your goals. To overcome identified barriers to your aspirations requires the application of the second framework, *Conquer Your Internal and External Interference*. Often, roadblocks and boundaries prevent us from living out our dreams. These interferences can be notably intrinsic or inherent to our genetic or psychological makeup, or they could result from extrinsic or outside influence from environmental, social, or economic factors.

The third framework is to *Act Intentionally to Achieve Your Goals*. This framework establishes the way forward on how you need to live your life daily.

I urge you not to let life just happen to you haphazardly. Instead, take intentional actions to realize your life goals and your purpose. Your goals may be many and varied at different stages of life, but it takes knowing yourself and reflecting on your experiences and shortcomings to truly dissect which goals really matter in fulfilling your divine purpose. Your proclamations, i.e., what you declare about yourself and circumstances, are pivotal in your ability to identify and overcome the interferences with your life goals. These interferences are explored throughout the chapters of this book, except for financial factors. You should strategically select choices in the direction of your dreams and goals to ultimately make changes to live your best life.

As you prepare to read this book, please get a writing journal to jot down your reflections and your responses to the probing questions. Also, get ready for introspection and a realignment of your life practices. I ask you to be open to adopting new perceptions and a new mindset. Let your intuition unveil and guide you through any hidden and underlying root causes, heaviness, cloudiness, or revelations that emerge. Know that God is vested in you, and He will direct your understanding to give you a glorious direction for your life.

Being a trained engineer, coach, and educator, I have mastered how to design solutions that solve problems, reduce waste, optimize a process or system, and improve efficiency or maximize profit. Also, as a faithful believer, goal-setting and fulfillment have always been intertwined in my life. My faith has been the recipe for my success as an educator, professional, daughter, aunt, sister, wife, and mother.

## PREFACE

The ***Goal Redeemer: 10 Principles for Overcoming Barriers to Achieving Your Goals and Fulfilling Your God-given Dreams*** book provides life benchmarks and establishes a path to reach your full potential. Be ready for an overflow of blessings in your life. I decree and declare that as you read this book, all past ways that have not served you will be unlearned, and new patterns will begin to form. Lean on the ultimate Goal Redeemer, Jesus Christ, and get ready for new victories!

Dr. Kemi Akintewe
Tampa, Florida

# PART I
# Know Thyself

*"Knowing God Helps You Know Yourself."*
—Rick Warren

# CHAPTER 1

## Practice Self-Reflection

*"Suppose one of you wants to build a tower. Won't you first sit down and estimate the cost to see if you have enough money to complete it?"* (Luke 14:28 NIV)

Standing outside my high school biology lab about three decades ago in Nigeria, I gazed out into the universe, thinking I would have a family, house, and reliable car by age twenty-four. That was all I could envision as a teenage girl growing up in Nigeria's busiest city, Lagos. Though I was born in the United States, I grew up in Nigeria. My parents were international students in the '70s and had my two older brothers and me while they were both in college. Soon after my parents graduated from college, they returned to Nigeria in 1980, and my younger sister was born there.

My perceived dream of getting married and starting a family was common among girls my age in West Africa. Our mothers and society groomed us to be dutiful wives and caring mothers by the time we graduated from high school or college, if our families were fortunate enough to afford the cost of higher institutions. Upon college graduation, young female adults are expected to bring home a marriage suitor. If they do not, the extended family members will also get involved in pressuring them. In the 1990s, I thought getting married soon after college graduation was a golden ticket to success. Then, I felt that it would be my ultimate accomplishment to complete my blissful story.

Well, my dream of having my own family didn't happen until almost two decades after high school. Regardless of the cards that life dealt me, subconsciously, my mind was keen on achieving that dream, even after realizing there was more to life than getting married and having children. Needless to say, I was naive and clueless about life and its challenges at that time. I thought life was straightforward, such that I could demand anything I wanted and receive it immediately just because I desired it and added it to my list of prayer requests. Not until I moved back to the United States in 1997 to start college in New York City did I gain a new awareness.

My relocation back to the United States changed my perspective on my dreams and aspirations. I was no longer limited by cultural beliefs, such as that women should be groomed only as wives and mothers. Nor was I at risk of being isolated or chastised for striving for professional success. With that awakening, I went on to study chemical engineering, a male-dominated field, and even earned a doctorate that I use to teach at a pre-eminent university.

Back then, in Nigeria, a woman being the breadwinner of her family was frowned upon. I saw a significant number of wives who downplayed their accomplishments or even denounced their accolades in an attempt to manage their husbands' fragile egos. I was amazed to see confident and high-achieving women in the United States who did not have to be defined by a man. I looked up to women like Oprah Winfrey, who helped families resolve conflicts and positively impacted millions of people's lives regardless of their marital status, age, gender, or race. Then, I started digging deeper in search of what I wanted to do in life and the type of impact I wanted to have on the world.

This awakening experience ignited my passion for teaching. One of the reasons I pursued a doctorate is to reach students from all walks of life and every part of the world. My training as a university professor has allowed me to serve humanity with the effect I want to have on them. My mission in life is to educate people to fulfill their God-given dreams without limits. I want to guide people toward realizing their full potential and living abundantly. I am fulfilled when I see my students earn their degrees, especially those with major challenges.

Reflecting on my younger years, I can say that my wishes back in Nigeria were only a dream, not a goal. Goals have developed plans. A goal without a plan is only a wishful dream. Of course, my intended goals were shaped by my culture, environment, experiences, and perceptions. Later in life, I realized that my goals had to be written down, professed, visualized, and SMART (specific, measurable, attainable, relevant, and time-bound) for them to be achievable. The SMART acronym is a goal-setting framework developed by George T Doran to guide the execution of tangible goals within a given period.

Write your personal mission statement. *What do you value? What is your vision?*

_____

_____

_____

*So, how can one practice self-reflection?* It is the careful, conscious thought about your experience and actions—an evaluation of your belief systems, character, motives, and behavior. Profound meditation on the Word of God is often required to initiate a self-reflective exercise. Many times in my life, when I get bulged down over a matter, I take time to meditate on the Scriptures before I take any action because I do not want my actions to be birthed from a place of anger. I remember Ephesians 4:26–27: "In your anger do not sin. Do not let the sun go down while you are still angry, and do not give the devil a foothold." I start by putting off anything that could hinder me, like negative thoughts, old habits, old ways, old places, and even old friends. "You were taught, with regard to your former way of life, to put off your old self, which is being corrupted by its deceitful desires; to be made new in the attitude of your minds; and to put on the new self, created to be like God in true righteousness and holiness" (Ephesians 4:20–24 NIV).

For meditation, I use worship music to relax, reduce anxiety, and clear my thoughts. I do not get out of this mode until I feel centered in Christ. Then I proceed to the Bible reading and prayers. This practice guides my self-reflection process to think deeply through different aspects of my life.

Before you move forward in striving for a goal, first examine whether your faith is genuine. "Examine yourselves to see whether you are in the faith; test yourselves. Do you not realize that Christ Jesus is in you—unless, of course, you fail the test?" (2 Corinthians 13:5 NIV).

Faith is the pillar and foundation for achieving our God-given goals. If you have wandered away from the faith, return to it, and follow the Lord. Consider these verses: "Let us test and examine our ways, and return to the Lord!" (Lamentations 3:40 ESV) and "I have considered my ways and have turned my steps to your statutes" (Psalm 119:59 NIV). Consistent faith through the valleys drives our goal to the finish line. When we feel like our goals are taking forever, we might get tempted to dabble in ungodly acts to cheat our way into achieving those goals. I find such situations as impermanent solutions often associated with consequences.

When we take shortcuts, we shortchange the full capacity of what the goal redeemer, God, can do in our lives. For instance, returning lost and found money to its owner might result in blessings beyond your imagination. I remember a time during church service when a man testified about how he and his wife were praying for money to help finish a project, and the husband found a stash of money in an envelope outside a bank. He thought that finding that money was God's way of answering their prayers. So he took the money home to his wife and came to church to share his good news. While sharing his testimony, the pastor interjected and corrected his understanding of God's nature. The pastor instructed him to return the money to the bank in the hope that they could locate the owner. In obedience, God resolved this man's financial issue by providing the proper means to complete his project with divine favors. So, God can carry all your burdens when you remain faithful in all circumstances.

Awareness of who you are, your experiences, and your pains helps you realize your makeup and the lens you use to view your life goals. During one of my reflections, I identified an unhealthy pattern I have used to relate to men. I experienced child molestation growing up in Nigeria. Around first grade, I remember a neighbor no older than twenty years old touching me inappropriately in our backyard. I felt so much pain. He held me so tight that I could not run away.

After he violated me, he gave me money without saying a word. What got me out of that incident that day was my mom calling me to find out where I was. I don't know why I couldn't tell my mom what happened. I was about seven years old and did not understand what those meant. Over the years, another neighbor did similar things, and I did not say or do nothing but comply. By the time I was sixteen, my first kiss was from someone I regarded as an uncle. When I was twenty-four years old, I visited Nigeria and ran into one of the child molesters at a function. He had the audacity to ask me to visit him after the event. At that point, I could have made a scene or told my parents, who heard the conversation and encouraged me to visit him. Running into him brought back memories of the pain I had buried during my years of relocation to the United States. I still had no voice. And the feeling of being voiceless began a pattern of distrust in men and a habit of insecurity in me. I thought less of myself and thought more of what others thought of me.

Reflecting on this experience has been the hardest thing for me, as I could not make sense of what was enacted upon me. I know the pain and torture of the experience built walls and affected having meaningful relationships with men. Nevertheless, I cannot give the adverse events in my life that much power to define or imprison me mentally. My wounds are not my labels. The enemy tries to use our pain as an instrument to terminate our dreams. Unconsciously, my wounds became my mouthpiece. I spoke and acted from my place of pain. No man could woo me. I viewed all men as abusers and never trusted any of them, especially family friends. All I could see were hidden agendas in their eyes whenever they tried to get close to me. I made a conscious decision to be guarded and never trust a man. Though I built these mental walls, losing my voice was a major barrier to success.

In order to heal from my experience, I needed me to remove barriers and open doors that had been shut. I cannot use this trauma to explain why I have been called a feminist, bitter, or an angry black woman. I look at other women who are called the same thing but have never faced molestation. But then I needed some answers. *Why was I their prey? Why couldn't I tell my mother or share my experience with my younger sister so she wouldn't fall victim?* None of my abusers threatened me if I told anyone. But still, I perpetuated the unspoken cultural norm of: "you don't talk about it." I kept it a secret for thirty years. It has influenced my decision-making and hindered my ability to present my authentic self. Unintentionally, I have re-victimized myself all these years. My true self had been hidden. My facial expression lines and demeanor tell of my trauma when I look at my photos from those years. Thank goodness for reflection. I was able to uncover my healing journey.

The answers to my questions were shameful. I felt ashamed. I blamed myself for not being able to voice my stance and say "no" to these men. And this blaming fueled my bitterness and how I related to the world. The problem was in my pattern of dealing with how the molestation showed up in my life. I had to unlearn the survival tactics I had built to cope so that I could heal and meet the man God had prepared for me. I have learned how to protect my spirit while being vulnerable enough to love and be loved. With this experience, I am more than a conqueror through Christ. And the same will be true for you in reflecting on and overcoming any past trauma you have faced.

**Self-inquiry Exercise**

*1. How have you felt when you have not been able to achieve a goal?* Please describe.

_____

_____

_____


*2. How is your current state of life in terms of satisfaction with how you live?* Please describe.

_____

_____

_____


*3. What are you doing daily to impact your goals?* Please describe your actions.

_____

_____

_____

*4. What is an outstanding goal that you are yet to achieve?* Write down one goal.

_____

_____

_____


*5. Does your outstanding goal align with God's Word?* Identify and write out that word of God from the Scriptures.

_____

_____

_____


Make your goals centered on God's words. When my friend Nancy and I started a Woman Empowerment and Building Group, our mission and vision were and still are anchored in the Scriptures. Through making decisions and planning topics to cover, we checked for agreements with the Word to ensure that they bring edification to Him and others. Your goal could be education, job, family, health, community, finances, or any other area of your life. Until I started writing down my goals and ensuring God's Word supported them, I started to experience repeatable results. As an engineering professor, one of my goals every semester is to teach fundamental concepts with tangible applications to everyday life. Whenever I struggle with a concept, I crosscheck to see if I have veered off from the objectives or goals, and then I make the necessary adjustments. This evaluative process has proven valuable and increased the rate of students who pass my courses.

Decide to take the appropriate steps to succeed in reaching your goals. Your goals should stem from your life's vision and mission. A clear vision will help determine the goals needed to reach your destination. Your goals must be written down if you want to accomplish them. I maintain a journal for writing all my annual goals and keep an endless list on my phone's Notes app.

A 2007 research study by Dr. Gail Matthews showed that you have a 42 percent chance of achieving your goals if you write them down, indicating there is power in simply documenting your goals in written form. I suggest you formulate and write out your ultimate goal first; this could be a lifetime achievement, followed by a long-term goal achievable within five to ten years. Then, write out your intermediate-term goals achievable within two to five years, followed by a short-term goal reachable within one to two years.

After identifying your short-term goals, the next step is to write down your immediate goals that are attainable in one year. Break your immediate goals into monthly or weekly chunks, then into daily goals. In a properly designed set of goals, your daily actions should reveal that you prioritize your immediate goals. For example, if you want to lose weight, your daily habits will show you eating healthy meals and consistently working out. If not, your apparent daily actions would predict an undesirable outcome incongruent with your long-term goals. Here is a template for a goal recording sheet I use for my coaching sessions.

## Goal Recording Sheet

*1. What is the **ultimate** goal that you desire to accomplish?*

_____

_____

_____

*2. What are your **long-term** goals (achievable in 5-10 years)?*

_____

_____

_____

*3. What are your **intermediate-term** goals (achievable in 2-5 years)?*

_____

_____

_____

*4. What are your **short-term** goals (achievable in 1-2 years)?*

_____

_____

_____

5. What are your **immediate** goals achievable within the next year?

_____

_____

_____

The foundation of an achievable goal is a robust plan. *What's your plan to achieve your goals? Are your plans SMART? Meaning, is your goal specific, measurable, attainable, relevant, and time-bound?* If your goal is to purchase a car, you must know what type of car you are looking for and have a budget for how much you are willing to spend. Then you have to be able to answer questions such as, *"Can I afford the car?" "How would I buy this car?" "Would I need a loan, or could I save a certain amount of money in a timeframe?" "By what date would I like to get this car?"* Whatever goal you've set for yourself, make it SMART, so it has a chance of being met.

Create four separate boxes and construct your Strengths, Weaknesses, Opportunities, and Threats (SWOT) analysis to evaluate any interference (internal and external factors) with your goals and determine a strategic plan for your SMART goals. During my job search days, I always included a personal SWOT analysis spreadsheet in my interview portfolio to highlight my strengths and weaknesses since that is a significant aspect of assessing compatibility. Also, I wanted to display a total image of how I could be an asset to the company or academic institution if given the opportunity. Although SWOT analysis was developed by Albert Humphrey for organizations, you can create one for individual purposes, as I do. For instance, if your goal is to lose weight, then your personal SWOT worksheet might look like this:

## Personal SWOT Analysis

### Strengths

**Q.** Which of your skills prepares you for this goal?

**Example:**
I have self-discipline. I participated in the last marathon with three months of preparation.

### Weaknesses

**Q.** What self-improvement can you make to enhance your goal?

**Example:**
I need to curb my eating habits and stop consuming unhealthy foods.

*Internal*

### Opportunities

**Q.** What knowledge, experience, or tools can help fulfill your goal?

**Example:**
I will sign up for a gym membership and hire a personal trainer.

### Threats

**Q.** What barriers or challenges might interfere with your goal?

**Example:**
My days are always full. Making time to work out will be challenging.

*External*

## Identify your SWOT

### Strengths

### Weaknesses

*Internal*

### Opportunities

### Threats

*External*

> *"Write the vision*
> *And make it plain on tablets,*
> *That he may run who reads it.*
> *For the vision is yet for an appointed time;*
> *But at the end it will speak, and it will not lie.*
> *Though it tarries, wait for it;*
> *Because it will surely come,*
> *It will not tarry."*
> (Habakkuk 2:2-3 NKJV)

---

**Moving Forward**

**Identify your roadblocks:** Have you always surrendered to self-defeat? Do you experience anxiety? Note that your accomplished goals are tied to other people accomplishing their goals. Your achieved goals will cause other people to realize their goals as well. The positive impact it brings breaks cycles and thus changes your generation and the future of those tied to you. Do the work now, and your future generations will benefit forever.

**Implement proven goal-setting frameworks:** Use the SMART goal model and the SWOT analysis tool to help realize your goals. Use a SWOT analysis template to assess your goal and identify the associated strengths, weaknesses, opportunities, and threats. The SWOT analysis reveals your potential roadblocks and helps identify the competencies that allow you to abound by listing the necessary skills and resources required to achieve that goal. Using the SMART model will help refine your goal after you have evaluated the interference, threats, and challenges to it.

CHAPTER 2

# Perform Self-Assessments

*"I thought about my ways and turned my steps back to your decrees."* (Psalms 119:59 CSB)

Reverend Sunday Adelaja's statement that "self-evaluation and assessment should be a major part of our lives as believers" is so true. Self-examination is similar to the principle of "counting the cost" to evaluate if you are fit for the goal. The prerequisite to accomplishing your goals is to practice frequent self-evaluation and authentic assessments during the different seasons of your life. Examine your achievements and aspirations.

Some people specialize in examining or judging others because it is much easier since it distracts them from looking inward and identifying their inadequacies. If you want to achieve your goals, you must regularly assess yourself. Practicing self-reflection, examination, evaluation, and introspection is necessary for personal growth and advancement in life and career. I attribute self-examination to accountability and honesty with yourself. To gain value and growth from introspection, you must be honest about whom and where you are.

After self-examination, you need to ask the Lord for the direction you should follow with your goals: "Search me, God, and know my heart; test me and know my anxious thoughts. See if there is any offensive way in me, and lead me in the way everlasting" (Psalm 139:23–24 NIV). The process of examining yourself helps reveal your offense in any given matter. Often, when an unknown action of mine angers my husband, I practice reflection. I reflect on our discussions and replay the scenes in my mind to help me understand my role and the root of his anger. Only then do I gain clarity.

Honestly assess your state of life. Ask yourself whether you are living your life the way you should—how God has purposefully designed it for you. In what areas of your life do you find fulfillment, and in what areas can modifying your routines or plans benefit you? As you move through your plans, ensure that you continuously review your goals, outcomes, and state of mind to analyze if they still align with your original vision.

> "The first step to personal growth is the ability to make an honest assessment of where you currently are."
> –Michell Pulliam

**Goal Assessment**

1. Think of your unachieved goals and state why you have been unable to reach them.

_____

_____

_____

*2. Have you been stuck at a point while working on attaining a goal?* Could you identify the roadblocks and barriers in reaching your goals? These roadblocks could be poor time management, people, fear, lack of motivation, habits, or impatience.

_____

_____

_____

*3. Can you identify the root cause of your barrier(s)?* Some common root causes may be the result of childhood trauma, poor habits, negative learned behavior, procrastination, lack of support, and limiting mindsets or perceptions.

_____

_____

_____

*4. If you identified more than one root cause, are there any similarities?* If yes, can you recognize any unproductive patterns between the root causes? You might want to use an app like "LifeCycle" for tracking patterns.

_____

_____

_____

5. Identify what is feeding your patterns or routines. Track your daily routine in order to try to pinpoint what is contributing to your pattern.

_____

_____

_____

*6. Can you identify one or two commonalities in your pattern?*

_____

_____

_____

After you conduct the Goal Assessment exercise, you can start to work toward breaking your identified unproductive patterns. Part II of this book provides a guide for overcoming barriers to fulfilling your goals.

**Relationship Assessment**

Ponder on your relationship with your parents. The nurturing we received or didn't receive during our formative "years" determines who we are today.

*1. What were the wounds you incurred as a child?*

_____

_____

_____


*2. What did you learn or not learn about goal setting?* Beware that some of the things you learned may now need to be unlearned.

_____

_____

_____


*3. What habits did you pick up from your parents about achieving or completing tasks on time?*

_____

_____

_____


I have witnessed parents who were not efficient with time management; their children picked up those habits and did the same thing when they had their own children. It becomes a cycle if you do not consciously try to break those habits. My father taught our family the value of time. During our high school days, my older brother, who was driven to school by him, was always at least half an hour early before the first bell rang. I believe my brother was disgruntled since he could have enjoyed some extra sleep, but now, he carries out the same practice with his children. I am the same way too. I prefer to arrive on time to professional gatherings to mingle with other early arrivers and settle down before the event starts.

*As an adult, how have you chosen to raise your children? How are you raising (or how have you raised) your children concerning their goals? Does it contrast or agree with the Word of God?* Use this opportunity to write out your goals for your children or modify your previously written ones as necessary.

If you are married or courting, evaluate whether your marriage or relationship is sacred. *How are you treating each other? Is your love or respect contingent on how the other person treats you?* Are you giving your all? What is your state of mind concerning your spouse? Write out your marital goals. Map out how you want your marriage to be. The Lord's design for marriage is to "Enjoy life with your wife, whom you love, all the days of this meaningless life that God has given you under the sun" (Ecclesiastes 9:9 NIV).

*At your job, are you a team player with your colleagues? Are you working hard to fulfill your roles and responsibilities?* Most importantly, *are you working hard as if you are working for the Lord? Do you have a professional and pleasant reputation with your supervisor and co-workers? Are you clear on the company's vision and mission?* If your work brings sadness rather than satisfaction, then you should take account of the whys and examine your future at that company. Where do you see yourself in five or ten years? Write out your career goals or modify your previously written ones if necessary.

*Are you a student in pursuit of a career or a new job?* Take your academic performance and long-term plans upon graduation into account. *Do you know where you are heading? Are you operating at your total capacity to get to your desired destination? What are your semester and yearly goals? How well do you relate with your peers in the same cohort? Do you have mentors and coaches in your life?* Use an individual development plan (IDP) template to examine your skills and strengths, set strategic goals, and pursue development opportunities for a career path. For science careers, the American Association for the Advancement of Science (AAAS) has created exercises to help guide you through the IDP process. In general, you want to develop your IDP by following these five steps:

1. Complete the Goal Recording sheet.
2. Identify your interests, strengths, competencies, and skills to be developed.
3. Discuss your response to step two with your career advisor and draft development opportunity plans suitable to address your interests and desirable skills.
4. Implement the plans in step three. This may require training, coaching, or taking certain courses toward your career goal.
5. Periodically evaluate your experience and development progression with your advisor.

*Ultimately, how is your relationship with God?* My secret to accomplishing every one of my goals lies in my intimate, personal relationship with the Lord. I consult with God about my goals. The Lord has prepared the tools necessary to work out all other relationships and bring your goals to life if you are willing to relate with Him and submit to His plan. God wants you to talk and walk with Him regularly. Assuming you have given your life to Christ, the goal redeemer, *how have you grown since making this decision?* "In fact, though by this time you ought to be teachers, you need someone to teach you the elementary truths of God's word all over again. You need milk, not solid food!" (Hebrews 5:12 NIV). *Do you still need milk instead of solid food? Are you still struggling with the same sin from your past? How often do you communicate with God? Can He call you His friend? Are you moving at the speed God desires of you, or has your pace been compromised? Are you spiritually sick? Have you fallen short because of sin?* Write and map out your spiritual goals.

Our habits and lifestyles change as we spend more time with the Lord. You get stronger and become strengthened by the Word of God, which also equips you to make effective decisions. People can live a particular way of life that brings sorrow, lies, selfishness, and greed to themselves and others. However, a life pleasing to God is peaceful, honest, loving, and joyful. People can do things that destroy their potential to live out their dreams and goals. Are you giving your all and doing your best to achieve your life goals? If not, why?

You are a true reflection of God's given potential. I challenge you to make life-changing goals that make you an inspiration and motivation to others, i.e., superiors, parents, children, colleagues, mentees, etc. Live a life that makes you a blessing and not a burden to others. To fulfill your destiny, you ought to consistently practice self-reflection to evaluate whether your goals, behaviors, and thoughts are in accordance with God's divine purpose for your life.

---

### Moving Forward

**Self-commitment**: The purpose of conducting a self-assessment is to initiate a personal growth path. Make a commitment to yourself that brings you closer to your goals. Be committed to burying old habits and forming new ones. Make daily commitments to win. Have a daily action plan. Know what you are supposed to do every day, even if it is planning a rest time. Do not let your day flow haphazardly. Start your day with gratitude and devotional practice. It grounds you and keeps you centered in Christ. Profess your daily desires with proclamations. Say today, "I will succeed in whatever I choose to do, and light will shine on the road ahead of me" (Job 22:28 NLT). Show up for yourself every time. Feel free to reset your expectations and leave room for re-calibration when situations get tough. Falling is inevitable, so plan for a comeback when it happens.

**Purposeful living:** Find out what you want and why you want it. Ask yourself, "What's *the purpose of this goal?*" Examine if you should change or stay the course. If what you want does not align with God's Word, restructure your plans so that it does. God is committed to bringing your heart's desires to pass if you ask according to His will. When you declare God's promises over your life, He remains true to His Word and will bring them to pass eventually.

**Personal assessments:** Conduct a critical assessment of your behavior and the general state of your mind to evaluate if they align with your life goals and God's will. To what extent are your goals in line with God's Word? Ask the Lord in your prayers to direct your path and establish your steps. "The heart of man plans his way, but the Lord establishes his steps" (Proverbs 16:9 ESV).

## Reflection Questions:

Take out time to reflect and address the following ten questions.

*1. What do you desire out of life?*

_____

_____

_____


*2. What are your dreams and aspirations?*

_____

_____

_____


*3. How do you see yourself achieving your goals?*

_____

_____

_____

*4. What have been the barriers to attaining your goals?*

_____

_____

_____


*5. Identify any old habits that you need to leave behind.*

_____

_____

_____


*6. What have you done about the hindrances to achieving your goals?*

_____

_____

_____


*7. What would you say you need now to help you achieve your goals?*

_____

_____

_____

*8. How do you want to feel when this goal is achieved?*

_____

_____

_____

*9. How would this goal uplift your soul and please God?*

_____

_____

_____

*10. How would this goal put you on a path of growth in a particular area of your life?*

_____

_____

_____

PART II

# Conquer Your Internal and External Interference

*"Even if good people fall seven times, they will get back up."*
(Proverbs 24:16a CEV)

### CHAPTER 3

# Principle 1
# Believe in Your Goals

*"Trust in the LORD with all your heart and lean not on your own understanding; in all your ways submit to him, and he will make your paths straight."* (Proverbs 3:5-6 NIV)

During my freshman year of college, back in the 1990s, I remember returning from campus to my apartment in New York City with a graduate school admission catalog from a university in the South. At that time, I had never been to the South or even left the Northeast. This catalog included a list of engineering graduate programs that exactly matched my interests. I sat on my approximately 250-square-foot bedroom floor and studied the admission requirements as if my life depended on it.

Shortly after, I started drafting a plan for getting into the graduate program of my choice. I wrote down the number of credit hours and types of courses I would need per semester and what grades I would need to earn to qualify for the graduate program. Keep in mind I was still only an undergraduate freshman. Unknowingly, I was setting goals. I have no idea what made me so driven, but it was clear I had it in me to succeed every step of the way to earn my master's and then a doctorate.

Along the way, I took classes and strategized how to excel in them. Unfortunately, some classes turned out differently than I originally planned. I remember crying after receiving a C in one of my major classes. I went to speak to the professor afterward, and he made me feel worse than I had felt for getting it. I am unsure if it was my stubbornness or my faith, but I became more determined to perform better after the insensitive encounter at my professor's office. Although I felt terrible, that grade did not make me quit or think less of myself. I had a tenacious mindset to fight for what I wanted. Then I pledged to commit to being successful and never let anyone or anything deter me. Still, I believed in my goal of being an engineer and continued to seek the path until I finally reached my goal of earning a doctorate in engineering, which I achieved fifteen years later. Regardless of the many obstacles that came my way, I was determined to pursue my goal.

Believing by faith that all our goals are achievable with God is pivotal to achieving those goals. Likewise, it is our premium access to Christ. John 3:16 says that whoever believes in Jesus will have everlasting life. Everlasting life is eternal life with Christ. In John 8:31–32, Jesus talked to the Jews who had believed in Him, and He persuaded them to continue to abide in His Word and know the truth that would set them free. Their belief in the Word qualified these Jews to be set free. You must align your life according to His Word. Your belief in the Word is the key to accessing your dreams.

Believing in Christ for your goals has significant benefits. When Jesus healed the woman with the issue of blood and resurrected Jairus's daughter in Mark 5:34–42, He mentioned to the woman that her faith had healed her (verse 34). He told the men from Jairus' house in verse 36, "Don't be afraid; just believe," and then the daughter came back alive.

If you believe, Jesus can even resurrect your lost dreams. In the story of the centurion's paralyzed servant, Jesus instructed the man to "Go! It will be done just as you believed it would. And his servant was healed at that very hour" (Matthew 8:13). In Matthew 9:27, Jesus asked the two blind men, "Do you believe that I am able to do this?" Once they answered yes, their sight was restored. What, who, and how you believe matter. Do you believe that with God, you can achieve your goals?

Faith in God and belief in yourself can catapult your goals to fulfillment even when you do not see an outcome or have empirical evidence of one. While my husband and I were trying to get pregnant, and we kept experiencing one miscarriage after another, I did not lose hope. Instead, I held on to the promises of God in Psalm 113:9 (NLT): "He gives the childless woman a family, making her a happy mother." And Deuteronomy 7:14: "You will be blessed more than any other people, none of your men or women will be childless, nor will any of your livestock be without young." When we finally had a fetus continue to develop into the second trimester, we experienced pre-term labor complications. I was on bed rest for two months. Throughout those weeks, I had unwavering faith that my goal of being a mother would come true. Indeed, the Lord came through for us, and He can do the same for you concerning your deepest desires if you believe.

Before giving birth to your goals, you must envision them and align your mind and thoughts with God's principles. And you must believe it will happen. "Ask and it will be given to you; seek and you will find; knock, and the door will be opened to you" (Matthew 7:7 NIV).

The first step is to ask, the second is to believe in whatever you ask, and the last step is to receive what you have asked and believed for. You don't want to practice one step without the other. If anyone says to this mountain, "Be removed," and has no doubt but believes that it will happen, it will be done (Mark 11:23). Believe what God says about your goals. He has plans "to prosper you, and not harm you, plans to give you hope and a future" (Jeremiah 29:11). The Lord will make you "the head, not the tail …, you will always be at the top, never at the bottom" (Deuteronomy 28:13). All things are possible for those who believe. Those who "know their God shall be strong and do exploits" (Daniel 11:32 KJV). Do you believe you can do great and mighty things? When we declare God's Words and obey them, He is committed to honoring them. Hebrews 6:12b states, "to imitate those who through faith and patience inherit what has been promised." God has a track record of keeping His promises and is not about to stop with yours. That is God's nature. He counts your belief in Him as righteousness. The God that can revitalize dry bones is still awake.

> *"Believe you can, and you're halfway there."*
> –Theodore Roosevelt

Growing up, I had a picket fence dream of having four children, a husband, a house, and a luxury car by a certain age. What I really wanted to achieve was a successful family life. Though I faced challenges along the way, I never lost faith in God's ability to see me through each of my preparatory and growing seasons. To God be the glory! I now have my white-picket fence house, a husband, two children, and reliable cars. Of course, with age and wisdom, I realized that I could not manage to have four children and accomplish my other goal of being a balanced career mother. I have learned that time and wisdom sometimes require that you adjust the original goal.

I understand that not everyone can relate to my faith experience or share my belief system. I have seen people who could not believe in their goals even though others could see that they had the materials, tools, and resources to support them. These people have embodied self-limiting beliefs that can block what the supernatural could do in their lives. It takes more than practical resources to believe in your goals. Embracing spiritual principles is crucial to redeeming your goals. The Israelites never changed their belief systems from their hand-made gods, even after they were delivered from their enemies, so they were not free. Sometimes we cannot achieve our goals because of our environment or the company we keep.

Be mindful of the people with whom you share your goals. Remember, you were the one God envisioned and assigned the goals to. People might not believe your goals because they cannot fathom God's plan for you. Others might even minimize your aspirations by laughing in your face or telling you they are too outlandish to achieve. Please don't be discouraged. Not everyone can handle what God has deposited in you. Your confidence could undoubtedly be chipped away when others don't believe in your goals. That's why I like professional coaches. They have the end in mind more than their clients and are there to prepare them mentally and physically to reach their goals. If you have tried to believe in yourself and nothing seems to be working, please seek assistance from a professional. Life coaches and therapists can help you remove mental blocks and self-limiting beliefs and reinforce a positive belief system.

> *"If you don't see yourself as a winner, then you cannot perform as a winner."*
> –Zig Ziglar

**Pathways to Believing in Your Goals**

Below are practices you should embody to walk on the path of believing in your goals:

**1. Remove your waste.** Identify what in your life needs to go in the trash. Could it be your sins, attitude, habits, self-defeating/limiting beliefs, fears, self-doubts, negative emotions, mindset, or even some people? If you walk with grouchy, negative people, eventually, their mindsets will rub off on you. "Do not be deceived, evil company corrupts good habits" (1 Corinthians 15:33 NKJV). If you surround yourself with goal-driven, ambitious, and positive individuals, you are bound to pick up their energies and mindsets. Sometimes, some people are not evil; they are just not good for you. Remove everything that hinders you from believing in your goals.

**2. Unlearn your limiting beliefs.** Every self-limiting belief about your life must be unlearned. These are preconceived notions and false accusations you've made about your strengths and abilities. For example, if you believe you can never get that promotion, you will likely act according to that belief, and your work performance might never be recognized. Replace every one of your "I can't" beliefs with "I can," and "I'm not" with "I am." You can do all things through Christ who strengthens you (Philippians 4:13), not some things but all things. "All things work together for good to those who love God, to those who are called according to His purpose"

(Romans 8:28 NKJV). Self-defeating beliefs stagnate you, and this is the enemy's agenda. Satan wants to destroy your goal at its inception. Don't fall for his tricks. Proclaim every one of the promises in your "I can" statement and replace your negative thoughts with positive ones and affirmations. Learn more about yourself, your goals, and the process of achieving them, then take action to acquire new beliefs and go into operation.

**3. Train your five senses to comply.** Consider looking at life with all your senses in full operation. Train your five senses to act according to what you want to receive. To "act" means to take *Action, Conquer, and Transform*. You should consciously monitor what you see, hear, touch, say, and smell to achieve your goals. Start your day by listening to uplifting music and motivational audible books or podcasts. Select the right type of movies to get entertained. Eating healthy foods is re-energizing and not depleting. Wear clean outfits, be well-groomed, and spray on reinvigorating fragrances that lift your mood. Be deliberate about the information processed by your senses. You want to train all your five senses to eliminate toxicity, negative imagery, or demotivating discussions.

**4. Put in your full efforts.** Life is full of challenges. You have the potential to fight the good fight of faith. Stand firmly anchored to the power of the Spirit and God's Word. Face your Goliaths and overcome them with your slingshot. Choose not to give up when it gets tough. Decide to work hard and spend time getting the results you want. The average successful business spends countless hours putting energy and time into refining its business model, products, or services before they reach a steady state. Focus on building your God-sized dreams and be determined to see changes despite any obstacles you may encounter. If you do nothing, nothing will happen. Work with all your might to succeed, and you will. Position yourself to win.

**5. Wear a positive attitude.** An approachable attitude is a prerequisite attribute to reaching any goal. Your attitude reveals your feelings, thoughts, and beliefs. A positive attitude is also a good predictor of your effort in achieving your goals. Your behavior can determine your potential to reach your goals. The inclination of your attitude sizes your goal potential. It is not the attitudes of others that establish your goals, but yours. Their attitudes can affect you, but you decide what to do with them. Manage your attitude. It is your responsibility and your asset. Others should have no control over your attitude. During every circumstance of your life, either good or bad, take charge and maintain a positive attitude. Our individual goals often depend on others; watch your reputation and treasure your attitude. Even if you cannot control a situation, ensure you control your attitude and respond wisely.

*"Believe in yourself. You are braver than you think, more talented than you know, and capable of more than you imagine."*
–Roy T. Bennett

---

**Moving Forward**

**Self-affirming words:** The words you speak are instruments for achieving your goals. Refrain from saying negative words about your goals and replace every self-limiting belief about yourself. For instance, instead of saying, "I can't pass this test," say, "I am victorious in any test I encounter." You must seek help if you need assistance stopping yourself from doing this and moving past it.

Meditate on the Scriptures that pertain to your goals. Write positive statements about your goals that are consistent with the Word of God. Make your affirmations measurable and actionable, such as: "I will be debt-free by the end of the year by paying off one creditor each month."

**Have faith:** It's time you release your faith to receive. God has lined up everything you need to be successful. Ask, seek, and you will find. You are not an impostor; believe in yourself. God has indeed created you for greatness. He wants to do beautiful things in your life. "Behold, the LORD's hand is not so short That it cannot save, Nor His ear so impaired That it cannot hear" (Isaiah 59:1 AMP). Do not let anything prevent you from accessing Him. Believe that you can do all things through Christ that strengthens you. That house that you want, the job that you desire, whatever it is, believe it is yours. Write down your goals and find the Scriptures that support what you believe will happen. Then recite the Scriptures when you pray.

**Positive behaviors:** You cannot change your behavior until you change your beliefs. You have no more excuses for why things haven't been working to help you reach your goals. Let your actions match a positive belief system. Your behavior reveals what you believe and informs others about your life. Start by listing three behaviors you want to incorporate into your daily habits and your strategy for doing so.

**Nurture your goals:** Let all your five senses be in tune to make your dreams come true. What you allow to influence your five senses are cursory entry pathways into your soul. You should smell successful, look smart, feel and live well, and be healthy and mindful. The sounds you allow in your life should be uplifting and boost your energy to achieve your goals. Write out the five pathways listed above and how you will execute them.

**Self-determination:** Take control of your life. Don't give up on your goals. God gave them to you because He can bring them alive. Go dig up all your past goals. He can breathe life into your dry bones. Be determined to put all your efforts into fulfilling those goals. Drop the victim mindset and put on the winner's hat. Purposely look for opportunities to feed your goals with life-affirming acts. List one or two things you are committing to do differently about your goals starting now.

# CHAPTER 4

# Principle 2
# Overcome Discouragement

*"Be strong and courageous. Do not be afraid; do not be discouraged, for the Lord your God will be with you wherever you go."* (Joshua 1:9 NIV)

There was a time in my life when I felt discouraged about completing my doctorate studies. I initially started pursuing my doctorate soon after my undergraduate degree. I was very enthusiastic about getting invited to a graduate open house at a university in the Midwest. It was not in my original plan to attend that graduate program. However, I agreed to visit since it was an all-expenses-paid trip. To my surprise, the program had a research topic area close to what I was interested in studying, so I left New York City in my 1993 Toyota Tercel and drove there to start a new life with no family or friends nearby. My courageous move lasted only a short time. It was a total culture shock. I had lived in busy cities all my life, and in this new state, getting things done seemed to take too long. To make matters worse, the graduate program was not diverse then. I was the only person of color in the whole graduate program for the first year.

This lack of diversity was not comparable to my undergraduate degree, where people of color were the majority. Academically, I struggled. It was hard for me to connect with my peers or the faculty. The more I tried to build camaraderie, the more discouraged I got. And the program advisor was incompetent and could not help me address the issues I was encountering. I felt alone.

Conversely, I was not getting moral support from the people in my life either. They said I did not need a graduate program and that an undergraduate degree in engineering should fetch me a decent salary. Unknown to them, I was not motivated by money but by a passion for teaching and conducting research, an opportunity that a PhD offers. Some people said that if I were "too" educated, no man would want to marry me. With the pressure of struggling in the program and listening to my naysayers, I left the program with a master's and found a job. I went against James Whitcomb Riley's wise words and allowed my enthusiasm to be dampened by discouragement. Of course, I returned to my senses and left my corporate job to go back and pursue my doctorate.

> *"The most essential factor is persistence—the determination never to allow your energy or enthusiasm to be dampened by the discouragement that must inevitably come."*
> –James Whitcomb Riley

Many years later, I discovered that most obstacles to achieving our goals are internal. Discouragement is one of the enemy's tools to distract and stop us from reaching our goals. When you feel discouraged, you may feel defeated, hopeless, worthless, sad, unconfident, or even insecure. These feelings, if not dealt with properly, can escalate to depression. Spiritually, discouragement affects our soul, body, and mind. You start to operate in low spirits, with little to no momentum or energy to perform your normal functions. In a state of inactivity, nothing can be accomplished.

Please answer the following questions to examine if you are in a state of discouragement.

*1. Have you lost hope that your goals can become a reality?* If yes, please elaborate.

_____

_____

_____


*2. Would you rather be by yourself?* If yes, please elaborate.

_____

_____

_____


*3. Which kind of people are you drawn to right now?*

_____

_____

_____

*4. Have you hit rock bottom and cannot see how to get out?* If so, please elaborate.

_____

_____

_____


*5. Do you feel trapped in an ordeal?* Please elaborate. If you are here, your goal should be to get out.

_____

_____

_____


To get out of discouragement, you need to identify what has stolen your joy, strength, willpower, and energy. This could be due to losing a loved one through death, divorce, or separation. Or it could be a bad medical report, postpartum issues, income loss, or a betrayal. Maybe you've given your all to a relationship, a career, or something else in the past, and it just didn't work out.

The King James Bible says David encouraged himself in the Lord (1 Samuel 30:6 KJV). "David was greatly distressed because the men were talking of stoning him; each one was bitter in spirit because of his sons and daughters. But David found strength in the Lord his God" (1 Samuel 30:6 NIV). Encouraging yourself might be hard to do, but it is possible. Regardless of what you are going through, God can do exceedingly abundantly above all you can think or imagine, according to His power within you. Give the season you are in some time and connect with God to get to where you want to be. When I received that unfavorable grade from my professor as a freshman, I was disappointed and discouraged by his attitude toward me when I went to him for assistance. I had to remember whose I am and know that I am whom God says I am despite my shortcomings or adversaries.

Second Corinthians 4:17 (ESV) says, "For this light momentary affliction is preparing for us an eternal weight of glory beyond all comparison." Your light affliction is for a moment, so focus on eternal glory. Whatever your situation, strengthen yourself in the Lord, like David did. No one did it for him but the Lord. With the Lord by your side, all things are possible. Stop dwelling on what caused the discouragement and halted your life goals. Instead, decide to leave the issues for Him to handle. Let your plans for the outcome of your goals encourage you.

If discouragement is not dealt with at the root, it can keep you stagnated from moving forward. When you are stagnant, no upward movement occurs, and your trajectory in life is halted. No progress can be made in one's health, job, marriage, parenting, or business. Instead, derailment, idleness, and sickness slip into one's life. Discouragement can escalate to serious health problems like depression and heart attacks if care is not taken. We have heard of people who commit suicide after losing their jobs or find themselves hopeless and discouraged about the progress they have not made in life. Discouragement is bound to happen; how we deal with it determines our wins.

It is necessary to take deliberate steps to overcome any discouragement deterring you from moving forward with your goals. Immerse yourself in the Word. Hebrews 4:12 says, "For the Word of

God is living and active. Sharper than any double-edged sword, it penetrates even to dividing soul and spirit, joints and marrow; it judges the thoughts and attitudes of the heart" (NIV). The Word of God is still living. It is not dormant or obsolete. Even though it was written many centuries ago, it is still relevant in the twenty-first century. Speaking the Word of God moves and changes lives. You can speak what you want into existence by proclaiming His Word. Faith, belief, and obedience should be in place as you declare His Word. God's Word cannot return to Him void without accomplishing His purpose. His Word always produces fruit.

Second Timothy 3:16 tells us, "All Scripture is God-breathed and is useful for teaching, rebuking, correcting and training in righteousness" (NIV). The Word is helpful for teaching and training so that we can learn. It is also relevant for rebuking and correcting what may be out of order in our lives. Letting the Word of God train you helps you stay in shape spiritually for every battle and obstacle you face and experience. You start to walk righteously, and if you get distracted, you go back to the Word to stay on track.

God encouraged Joshua, after the death of Moses, to lead the Israelites to cross the Jordan River into the Promised Land with courage. "Have I not commanded you? Be strong and courageous. Do not be terrified; do not be discouraged, for the Lord your God will be with you wherever you go" (Joshua 1:9 NIV). *Are you discouraged because someone who helped raise you or mentored you is gone? Or do you have a challenging task ahead of you?* Be strong and practice courage. The Lord is with you.

Discouragements are the enemy's schemes to keep us from reaching our goals. Recognize what Jesus did in the wilderness when the devil tried to tempt Him. Jesus was able to dismiss the devil because He knew the Word of God. Luke 4:1-2, 8, 12 tell us, "Jesus, full of the Holy Spirit, left the Jordan and was led by the Spirit into the wilderness, where the devil tempted Him for forty days. He ate nothing during those days, and in the end, he was hungry." "Jesus answered, "It is written: 'Worship the Lord your God and serve him only.'" Jesus answered, "It is said: 'Do not put the Lord your God to the test.'" The Word of God strengthened and empowered Him. Learn from Jesus' response to Satan. He was not dismayed; instead, He fought Satan with the Word of God.

Trust in the Lord and be patient with Him to lighten your yoke and the burden that discouragement has brought you. It took twenty-five years for God's promise to make Sarah a mother to be fulfilled. Though Sarah did not believe so, she took matters into her own hands and gave her maidservant, Hagar, to her husband, Abraham, to conceive an heir. Sarah regretted her actions, and Hagar had to run away from her to avoid Sarah's mistreatment. God's promise to Abraham and Sarah that "she will be the mother of nations" (Genesis 17:16 NIV) came to pass.

I know many women who could not conceive for years, and later God blessed them with twins or triplets. It pays to wait for God to act patiently. The Lord promises to pay back your lost years and finish the good works He started. Have faith in the Lord to bring His Word to pass concerning that matter. Challenges work for us, not against us, preparing us for what is yet to come. God promised not to give you more than you can handle. He orders every one of your steps. Trust that He will fulfill His purpose for you and set you up on a solid foundation.

God will encourage us when we seek His face. I remember being discouraged during my doctoral study and crying to the Lord. As I was about to pray, He led me to 1 Corinthians 2:9 (NLT), which says, "No eye has seen, no ear has heard, and no mind has imagined what God has prepared for those who love him." Whenever I feel discouraged and remember this Scripture, I smile because I know God loves me and has a glorious plan for my future.

Godly perception is inevitable when a person is filled with His Word. Perception is formed by what you know. Be optimistic! See the good in every situation. For example, if you have a possession taken away from you, it could be that God is protecting you from future heartaches. Do not take revenge; the Lord will fight your battle for you. Vindication is for Him.

No matter how huge your mountain is, God can move it. He is our conqueror. Remember that "greater is He who is in you than he who is in the world" (1 John 4:4 NASB). In the meantime, fix your eyes on what is unseen, since what we see is temporary, but what is unseen is eternal (2 Corinthians 4:18). We have all we need to overcome the perils of this world because God has given us the authority. "I have given you authority to trample on snakes and scorpions and to overcome all the power of the enemy; nothing will harm you" (Luke 10:19 NIV).

Let God guide your perception. Please do not rely on yourself to work it out. First Samuel 2:9 (KJV) tells us, "For by strength shall no man prevail." Say, "This too shall pass."

*After you are filled with God's words, what can you do?* Trust Him and exercise patience. It might be necessary to change your attitude and environment too. Practice worshipping the Lord even when you are low or don't see a change. He is working things out on your behalf.

Be mindful that victory awaits on the other side. You may be a few days away from God fulfilling your goals. Praise God amid discouragement. Profess only positive things; proclaim them even when there seems to be a dark cloud. Be careful what you say. Keep your mouth shut if you do not have anything uplifting to share. Hold on to God's Word and speak from that only, not from man's words.

Instead of sadness, demonstrate that you have joy because you are coming out of a challenging season. Don't be downcast. Don't listen to the voices of other people; listen to God. He lives in you. Don't begin to blame God in your hour of darkness. Jesus has defeated every one of your dark moments. Let your praise increase instead.

Remember the story of Elijah and Jezebel in 1 Kings 19? Elijah ran for fear of Jezebel and asked God to let him die. Please don't give up or condemn yourself; your victory is near. Remind yourself that God has a solution before the problem arises. The devil wants to frustrate you so that you will give up. Your attitude should be that God will not allow this unless it is part of His divine purpose. It is a setup to show others His greatness and display His power.

No weapon formed against you shall prosper. View your circumstance as an opportunity to display God's glory. He wants to turn your test into a testimony. Remain connected even during your troubled times. Look at your situation as a step closer to your destiny. It may not seem visible naturally, but trust that all things are working out for your good spiritually.

Everyone has been discouraged at one time or another. My situation with my engineering professor in the *Self-Motivation* chapter could have discouraged me from continuing in that discipline, but I did not let it disempower me. Having a faith-affirming belief system on how to deal with discouragement is what you need.

*Are your excuses for not achieving your goals because of how the system operates? Or how you sound, look, or talk? Maybe it's what you don't have or how you are being perceived. Or do you say no one understands you?* Stop! "Trust in the Lord with all your heart; do not depend on your own understanding. Seek his will in all you do, and he will show you which path to take" (Proverbs 3:5–6 NLT). Keep declaring the Word concerning your situation. "God is not man, that he should lie, or a son of man, that he should change his mind. Has He said, and will He not do it? Or has He spoken, and will He not fulfill it?" (Numbers 23:19 ESV). I tell you, as long as God is alive (and He is eternal, so He is always alive), your tomorrow shall be greater than today.

---

**Moving Forward**

**Acquire affirming words:** Write down your goals in these areas: relationship, finances, personal growth, spirituality, children, education, business, and any area of need. Search for scriptures that address those areas. Use those scriptures as prayer points. Put the scriptures to memory and recite them whenever you feel discouraged. There will be times when you don't have your Bible, and the memory of the Word will keep you. Acquire images of your affirming words and post them everywhere. You can purchase framed Scripture wall art for your living spaces. Take some time to find and write down your affirming words.

**Act courageously:** Deliberately decide to act with courage in the area that causes you to be discouraged. Consciously take brave steps that demonstrate the change in your outlook and actions. Test yourself with smaller tasks and then build yourself up gradually. Be determined to fight the good fight to become victorious. Write down the one area you want to work on and state the courageous act you will take today.

**Pray:** Ask that the spirit of discouragement be broken in your life. Ask God to strengthen your inner mind so you can walk in the spirit of courage. Ask God to break the spirit of hopelessness, depression, and discouragement in every area of your life. Pray for an inner filling with the spirit of courage to overcome whatever is holding you back. Add these points to your prayer list and write any additional ones you desire.

**Seek help**: If you feel discouraged after implementing all these strategies, please seek professional support. A professional can work with any underlying issues you may have and assist you in getting to a better place. Start by talking to trusted allies for recommendations and commit to following through.

CHAPTER 5

# Principle 3
# Forgive Yourself and Others

*"It is to one's glory to overlook an offense."*
(Proverbs 19:11 NIV)

In 2017, I learned about Sarah Montana, a 22-year-old woman who forgave her mother and brother's killer. The killer was a 17-year-old kid who was her friend's younger brother from her neighborhood. He had shot them because he was caught stealing snacks from their kitchen cabinet. Sarah had compassion for her family's killer, forgiving him after seven years of being incarcerated on a life sentence. She realized the Bible had sixty-two passages on the word "forgive" and another twenty-two on the word "forgiveness," but she could not find how to forgive. Then Sarah realized her real problem was not how, but why she needed to forgive. She knew the Scriptures well enough to know it was the right thing to do, but her "aha!" moment came when she discovered that forgiveness sets the victim free.

*"The weak can never forgive. Forgiveness is the attribute of the strong"*
–Mahatma Gandhi

Forgiveness is a path to freedom and leads to a life open to abundance. Perished dreams and goals are bound to happen where unforgiveness reigns. Relationship goals are abolished when the relationship is terminated due to a lack of forgiveness. There are different facets of unforgiveness. All in all, forgiveness is a commandment, and if not done, it will affect your relationship with God, yourself, and others. *How should one approach forgiveness?* Know that forgiveness is a healing process, and restoration is another process. You cannot forgive merely with willpower; you need God's divine power and grace. Forgiveness gives accommodations for wrongs or pains. It moves past an offense and does not expect the past to be rewritten or changed to something better than it was.

Forgiveness of self means you genuinely believe that God has forgiven you. You might not forgive yourself for your errors or lost and failed goals. How can unforgiveness be a distraction from achieving your goals? To forgive means you have chosen to give grace and forbear. It begins with a motion or movement toward letting go of the hurt. When you are focused on achieving a goal, along the way, offenses knock at your door, looking for a way to derail you from accomplishing whatever mission God has placed in you. The key to reaching your full potential is recognizing distractions and not getting swallowed by them.

> *"As unrelated as it may seem, the fact is that forgiveness is the first step toward reaching all other goals. Without it, all the actions we take in other areas of our lives are stifled. It is impossible to fully engage in any other goal if we are harboring anger, resentment, or regret. When we hold on to emotional hurts from our past, we limit our ability to embrace our more tangible goals. Our goal should first improve our spirit, and then we can improve our circumstances."*
> –Cynthia Corsetti

Unforgiveness prevents us from experiencing breakthroughs. It is like carrying a burden or a weight that slows you down from moving toward your targeted goals because the power you need to accelerate in life can be tied to unforgiveness. You must first forgive yourself so that you can move forward. Could it be that you have not forgiven yourself for committing adultery or having an abortion? God can heal that wound. I have had my share of self-forgiveness. The hardest one for me was terminating what would have been my firstborn child. I named him Anu (meaning mercy in the Yoruba language). Yes, I believed that he was a boy. I had just earned my undergraduate degree and discovered I was pregnant a few months after the ceremony. There was no way it was true. I frequently missed my periods, so that was not my clue. My body felt very different, so I bought a ten-minute home pregnancy test from a faraway pharmacy store, trembling and thinking, "God, please make this negative. I will never live in disobedience anymore if you do me this one favor."

I had so many dreams to accomplish, and I did not think I could do it with a child. At that time, I lived rent-free in New York City with my two brothers, who paid the bills. And I was just starting to interview for jobs all over the country. I had all the excuses for not wanting to keep the child. Without discussing it with the man who fertilized my egg or giving him a chance to have an opinion, I performed the abortion. I would tell myself that Anu would have been this age year after year. I wonder how he would have looked, and there are times when I would not want to remember him or wonder what life would have looked like with him in my life. I lived with the secret for a decade until I married Tunde, and we could not have a child. That was when I reflected on the abortion and thought maybe that was God's way of calling my attention to dealing with my past. So, I asked my husband for a ride to a public night park.

There, I shared the secret with him. I was surprised that he was calm and did not judge me. I slept so well that night and for many nights after. The enemy could no longer use that sin to demonize me. I have sought the Lord's face. He had already forgiven me, but now I have forgiven myself, and I am free from the guilt and shame I associated with my abortion.

Unforgiveness has much more to do with the wronged individual than with the offender. It is commonly described as drinking poison but expecting someone else to die. If unforgiveness occurs, it can result in bitterness, rage, unhealthy habits, stress, heartaches, headaches, addictions, selective memory recall of hurts, cancer, anger, and even depression. *In what area of your life are you experiencing unforgiveness? Has someone offended you? Are you struggling to forgive yourself, your parents, children, siblings, other family members, friends, coworkers, ex-partners, or strangers?*

*Does the significance or depth of the offense matter? Could it be abuse, neglect, or violence?* Could you be stuck in your past hurts or failures? Identify the offense, offender, and where you are stuck in pain. Then permit yourself to enter a new beginning.

> *"Lord, how many times shall I forgive my brother or sister who sins against me? Up to seven times? Jesus answered, I tell you, not seven times, but seventy-seven times."*
> (Matthew 18:21-22 NIV)

Forgiveness is a commandment (Matthew 6:12), but it's also unnatural. Unforgiveness is a learned behavior. It is toxic, and it corrodes and robs you of your future. It prevents you from focusing on your tasks, thus keeping you from reaching your goals. Unforgiveness can bring about sleepless nights and hinder your prayer life, worship, and relationships.

Get rid of your pride or need to avenge the offender. Otherwise, you will become engulfed in the offense and unable to escape the pain. Neither will you be able to grow spiritually. Unforgiveness causes us to lose authority over Satan. He uses the offense as a device or scheme to set you back. Importantly, you do not want to help Satan execute his goal to steal, kill, and destroy.

Forgiveness does not excuse the offense or the offender, but rather allows the offended to find peace. So how do you deal with forgiveness when you are the offender? My marriage to my husband, Tunde, did not start out rosy. Even though I married a family friend with whom I shared similar life experiences, we are very different. Tunde went on to the military; he worked as an Air Force electronic engineer, and I worked in Virginia as an aerospace materials engineer for a defense company. We just so happened to be driving the same luxurious car when we met through our fathers in 2008. On Saturday, December 8th, 2007, I was going to drop my Dad off at the Baltimore airport when we ran into Tunde's father, who was dropping off his uncle. He asked my Dad who this beautiful lady was, and my father responded, "Miss World (a nickname my parent's friends gave me), my first daughter. You met her when she was only a few months old." My father-in-law responded jokingly, saying, "I have two handsome sons in Florida who are bachelors." At that point, I tuned out their conversation, only to find that my Dad later gave him my phone number. Two and a half years after that meeting, Tunde and I married.

*Can two walk together unless they agree?* Although we both worked as engineers, had similar interests in cars, and had excellent credit scores, these commonalities were insufficient to lead to a successful marriage. I love the things of the Lord; I could spend ten hours in church per week while Tunde was far removed from any religious activity.

Unscriptural, I made decisions without talking about them with him. I would share my final decisions without trying to gain his input. After my doctoral studies, I wanted to go to Boston for postdoctoral studies. So, I informed him and went with our two young children, leaving him alone in Florida. Throughout my almost two years away, I did not think of how he felt about taking our kids, who were under the age of two at that time. Returning to Florida, he was excited about reuniting with his children but not with his wife. I got the cold shoulder and snarky remarks. There was just so much built-up anger that we lived as roommates. Unbeknownst to me, I had no clue why he was so hostile toward me. When I got fed up with his attitude, I went on my knees to ask God for guidance. "If my people, which are called by my name, shall humble themselves, and pray, and seek my face, and turn from their wicked ways; then will I hear from heaven, and will forgive their sin, and will heal their land" (2 Chronicles 7:14 ESV).

So, on one fateful Sunday, as I was getting ready to leave for church, I made an appointment to meet with him later that day. In the past, these meetings entailed me coming up with a list of different items on the agenda and me posing accusatory questions. Tunde would respond with his guard up, and an attitude like, "What else do you want me to do, woman?" But this time around, I approached our meeting differently. After church service, I asked one of the elders to pray about my heart's heaviness and marriage. Once I returned home, in the driveway, I prayed again for the Holy Spirit to guide me, and then I spoke to Tunde with humility, admiration, and wisdom. I cannot remember what I said exactly, but the conversation led him to open up about all he had been harboring over the years about me. Tunde felt like I did not respect him. I was surprised, but I decided to listen attentively and not attempt to defend myself.

Without it being said, I knew by the end of our meeting that Tunde had forgiven me. We discussed what respect looks like for both of us and redefined our roles and expectations in the marriage. That was how our marriage was restored from unforgiveness.

We do not forgive because the person deserves forgiveness. Release people from unforgiveness so that you can move past it. Do not let the offense be stronger than you, so much so that you become bitter and it controls your mood and actions. Forgiveness is for the strong. It shows that you know people are not above making mistakes. Be mindful that unforgiveness can inhibit growth. Some people have been unable to climb the corporate ladder or gain ground in their marriage, career, education, or relationships because of unforgiveness. Don't let that be you. Be committed to yourself that no one will ever get you to the point where they hold your peace hostage. Focus on your destination, and don't let anyone slow you down because of unforgiveness. Cast down all imaginations of the offense. The enemy will use people to distract you, but the Lord will place people strategically in your path to propel you to prosper and fulfill your goals. The right people will be like branches connected to the true vine, lifting you and preparing pathways for you to flourish. Apostle Chibuzor Chinyere rightfully states that unforgiveness chains you to the past, poisons your present, and frustrates your future. Don't let anyone or anything keep your blessings from you. Forgive the inexcusable, even if there are no justifiable reasons. Forgiveness is mercy, not justice. However, forgiveness does not mean being foolish. If you have forgiven your molester, that does not warrant allowing your children to be around a sex offender unsupervised. Be wise.

Paul David Tripp, the author of *"What Did You Expect? Redeeming the Realities of Marriage,"* states that forgiveness is a *vertical commitment* followed by a *horizontal transaction*. If you are committed to the goal redeemer, God, you will be equipped with the necessary tools to help relate to one another.

The Scriptures provide guidelines on how to develop a forgiving spirit. It would be best if you strived to live peacefully with all men. Let go of everything that hinders you. The CEV Bible version puts it very nicely. "So, we must get rid of everything that slows us down, especially the sin that just won't let go. And we must be determined to run the race that is ahead of us" (Hebrews 12:1 CEV).

Ephesians 2:31–32 also elaborates on what to get rid of, such as anger, bitterness, slander, and malice. Forgive people's wrongdoings. In Proverbs 19:11 (NKJV), we are instructed to be slow to anger and overlook an offense. The NLT version says you earn respect when you can withhold wrath. Imitate God in how He forgives and how Christ taught His disciples to forgive (see Colossians 3:12–13 and Matthew 18:21–22).

Humbly grant forgiveness. "God resists the proud, But gives grace to the humble" (1 Peter 5:5b NKJV). Practice true love. "Love is patient, and love is kind. It does not envy, and it does not boast. It is not proud. It does not dishonor others, and it is not self-seeking. It is not easily angered, and it keeps no record of wrongs. Love does not delight in evil but rejoices with the truth" (1 Corinthians 13:4-6 NIV). Pray for God's power to move you in the right direction. Refrain from asking God to avenge your offenders and deal with them; instead, ask Him to give you a forgiving spirit.

To achieve your goals, you must set and enforce healthy boundaries to prevent the recurrence of an offense. Let your boundaries be set out of love, and focus on the motive. Decide to release the emotional burden of unforgiveness and experience joy and freedom. Do the work. Try the scientifically proven method developed by Dr. Robert Enright, his four-phase Process Model of

Interpersonal Forgiveness. Phase 1: Uncovering one's anger; Phase 2: Deciding to forgive or be forgiven; Phase 3: Working on forgiveness, and Phase 4: Deepening phase—discovery and release from emotional prison.

During the work phase (Phase 3), use practical steps as described in the late Dr. Wayne Dyer's blog, "How to Forgive Someone Who Has Hurt You: In 15 Steps." Use Enright's forgiveness model roadmap to work out your hurts and ultimately seek a breakthrough from God.

> **Moving Forward**
>
> **Reflection:** Think of the goals you have not been able to accomplish. Reflect on areas where you may harbor resentment, bitterness, and a lack of forgiveness in your relationships with family, yourself, or others. *Are there any forms of grudges or blame involved? Do you bring up past events in arguments? How old are these feelings?*
>
> *Are there patterns of behavior that continue to offend you? Are you willing to push yourself to forgive?* You may be standing in the way of reconciliation if you've never taken responsibility for your part of the problem. Seek forgiveness from others. Make a list of these and resolve to be free of the wrong and pain.
>
> **Self-forgiveness:** *Have you violated your values or standards? Are you experiencing guilt?* If you are still angry and disappointed in yourself, decide today to let it go. Give yourself the gift of forgiveness. You deserve to be forgiven, regardless of the magnitude of your offense. We serve a God of multiple chances. Don't give the enemy a permanent place in your heart because of your weakness. Make

declarative statements about how God has already forgiven you. For example, state the following as you start your day:

- Because of Christ's redemption, my sins are washed away, I am a new creature in Christ.
- I am no longer trapped or defined by my past. I step into God's grace and walk in total freedom and restoration. I reign in peace and joy.
- I am in total harmony with God's words.
- I welcome new experiences rooted in love, peace, and joy.

**Self-acceptance:** Accepting yourself is crucial to self-forgiveness. Break down any walls within yourself and practice self-love and acceptance. Give yourself the gift of forgiveness so you can focus on your goals. Discover who you are.

*"I don't trust people who don't love themselves and tell me, 'I love you.' There is an African saying which is: 'Be careful when a naked person offers you a shirt.'"*
–Maya Angelou

**Be an olive branch:** Enter a space conducive to achieving new goals. Be tolerant and forbearing. At times, the offender does not even know or care. *What have you done deliberately to open your heart to forgiveness?* Love and respect yourself enough to tell yourself and others the absolute truth about you. Have faith in yourself! *Are your actions in alignment with the Word of God?* Decide to make amends today, whether you are the offender or not. Stop harboring unforgiveness. Reach out and have those tough conversations. End on a positive note, no matter what.

**Prayer points:** God promises you an abundant life. *How can you receive it if you still hold on to past hurts?* Spend time in prayer for those who have hurt you. Get rid of it so you can receive what He has prepared for you. LET IT GO so that you are free to birth your future.

Ask God to bless you with a forgiving spirit and for healing and restoration of things lost or experienced due to unforgiveness. Plead for God's power to move you in the right direction and for the power to unlearn this destructive behavior of unforgiveness.

Pray for the wisdom to relieve the pain of self-forgiveness. The enemy will bring flashbacks, so be prepared to bind them. Repent of unforgiveness. Break every chain of unforgiveness that has kept you in one spot and prevented you from moving forward. For anyone who has refused to forgive you, ask the Lord to release you and have mercy on you. Ask the Lord to recover everything that you have lost to unforgiveness. Ask the Lord to wipe away every one of your wrongdoings.

Pray for the strength and courage to purge all resentments, both those you remember and those you don't. Ask for courage to do God's will.

# CHAPTER 6

# Principle 4
# Overcome Your Fears and Walk in Boldness

*"Do not fear [anything], for I am with you; Do not be afraid, for I am your God. I will strengthen you, be assured I will help you; I will certainly take hold of you with My righteous right hand [a hand of justice, of power, of victory, of salvation]."* (Isaiah 41:10 AMP)

Ever since my first summer internship in New Orleans, I became aware that I had anxieties and fears about speaking in groups, especially when it came to oral presentations. During the mid-term evaluation, we had to give an oral report of our project status. I remembered sweating profusely and then hyperventilating. I dreaded talking in groups. All these years, I have thought maybe it was solely because of my African accent or because I suffered from imposter syndrome. Imposter syndrome is the severe doubts of one's skills, talents, and accolades. The person feels like a fraud in their professional space. It could also mean the inability to accept your accomplishments even though you have the credentials to show for them. But my assumptions about the root of my fears were wrong.

During one of my visits to a therapist, I uncovered an event that happened in middle school. I was in the drama club, and we had rehearsed the Christmas recital numerous times. However, when it was my turn to speak, I forgot my lines, and the crowd booed me. My fellow cast members tried to help me by whispering my lines, but I still did not get them. As a young girl, around eleven years old, I subconsciously harbored the fear of speaking in groups for decades after that incident.

Fear is a common factor. Do you know that the most repeated phrase in the Bible is, *"Do not be afraid?"* So much that it is mentioned over 350 times in some Bible translations. The King James Version of the Bible has five hundred references to fear alone. The frequency indicates that everyone will wrestle with fear. Some elements of fear are more prominent than others, but the area of your fear is where God desires to empower you to reach your full potential. The Oxford Dictionary defines fear as an "unpleasant emotion caused by the belief that someone or something is dangerous, likely to cause pain or a threat." Most times, fear affects how you see people, treat others, and conduct your life, and most importantly, it impacts your relationship with God. Fear alters your behavior and can lead you to hide, run away, or freeze in your tracks. I call fear a terrorist. *Who or what is your terrorist? What is that one thing that keeps you up at night, consumes your day, and impedes your growth spiritually, physically, or mentally?*

Fear is a physical or emotional response to threats. Traumas or bad experiences can trigger fear, often defined as your "demons." Whatever your source of fear, the spirit of fear is not from God. He uses the enemy's toolbox to stop you from moving forward with your goals. Luke 10:19 (NIV) says, "I have given you authority to trample on snakes and scorpions and to overcome all the power of the enemy;

nothing will harm you." The Scripture says we have been set free from fear, but that does not necessarily mean the disappearance of it. But when it arises, we have been given the authority to rule over it.

The actor Bruce Lee said, "To understand your fear is the beginning of really seeing." Fear can blur your vision. You become unable to visualize the glorious destiny that God has for you because you have allowed fear to suppressed it. Fear has been my main obstacle to achieving my goals. I had all the possible reasons that I told myself were true. I was always the only female working on an engineering project. I feared I was never understood. I made many assumptions about what people thought of my technical contributions. And I experienced imposter syndrome. I lied to myself that I was not wanted or needed at work and was hired based on affirmative action, even though I was getting outstanding annual reviews and awards.

The enemy had me so afraid that my goals became secondary. He only needed to instill fear in my life to change my trajectory. The way I was raised was a factor. Being bold was considered rude, and trusting others was nonexistent. I grew up being super vigilant and paranoid about life. I perceived my upbringing to be pessimistic about people living their authentic selves. Until a few years ago, I hadn't realized that the spirit of fear was in full operation in my life. It took seeking help and reflecting on my productivity at work, relationships, and whole life to realize this. The enemy will do to you whatever you permit.

**Every other spirit works off the spirit of fear.** I was delivered from fear when I researched the topic and preached it at a church service. I would say I am still a work in progress. When fear wants to show up, I go into my toolbox and pull out my weapons of destruction—faith, boldness, self-discipline, love, and the power to extinguish any flames.

Fear can block the flow of the Spirit. "For this reason, I remind you to fan into flame the gift of God, which is in you through the laying on of my hands. God gave us a Spirit not of fear but of power and love and self-control" (2 Timothy 1:6-7 ESV). Timothy may or may not have struggled with intimidation; however, Paul reminded him to stir up and cultivate the gracious gift of God already living inside him, which is activated by the Spirit of power, love, and a sound mind. Please do not allow your goals to lay dormant by fear rekindle every one of those dreams that God deposited in you. Now is your season to make a magnificent shift and start manifesting the gifts laid inside of you.

Many people have lost their dreams and the ability to fulfill their purpose in life because of fear. The mandate from God is to overcome fear. Many people are bound by fear, and it enslaves them. Hebrews 2:14–15 (NIV) states, "So that by his death he might break the power of him who holds the power of death that is, the devil and free those who all their lives were held in slavery by their fear of death." The devil does not want your materials and possessions, but he will take them away if they have the potential to rob you of your peace and joy. Some people cannot enjoy their hard-earned materials because they fear losing them.

> *"Our greatest glory is not in never falling but in rising every time we fall."*
> –Confucius

Why destroy fear? Because fear takes you to a state that decapitates and holds you back from living your God-given dreams and achieving your goals. However, some level of fear might serve our goals, but I am not talking about such fear. I am referring to the fear that paralyzes you and inhibits goal manifestation. The devil wants to mask your fear with timidity, anxiety, or a problematic lifestyle to lead you to unfruitfulness.

Doubt in oneself and one's abilities is a major deterrent to wanting to lift a finger to accomplish anything. In Mark 11:22–23 (NLT), the Scripture says, "Have faith in God. I tell you the truth, you can say to this mountain, 'May you be lifted up and thrown into the sea,' and it will happen. But you must really believe it will happen and have no doubt in your heart." Fear shakes your confidence in God and replaces it with doubt. It says you will never achieve your goals because you don't have the skills, don't deserve this or that, or no one will believe you or want you. I heard Bishop T. D. Jakes say, "Don't let the pain of your past bleed into your present and poison your future."

Anxiety is barricaded by fear. If not dealt with, fear can lead to depression. You must conquer your fears if you truly want to be free. Jesus said, "So if the Son sets you free, you will be free indeed" (John 8:36 NIV).

> *"Never trust your fears, they don't know your strength."*
> –Athena Singh

**Eleven Types of Fear**

Many of us fear dying, getting sick, losing our jobs, being unable to pay our bills, or being replaced. Fear is gripping us, choking us. Fear will lead us to make unscriptural, illogical, irrational, and ungodly decisions. It can severely handicap you from doing God's will. Which of these dimensions of fear grips you?

**Type 1: Fear of others.** Fear of people can prevent you from reaching your goal. Who are you afraid of? Some people have made you believe that your life is in their hands, so you are afraid to leave or embark on your dreams. It is dangerous when we are always concerned about the opinions of others. Growing up, I always heard the older generation say that *advice does not cost a red cent.* Don't get me wrong; there is wise counsel and counsel that is not so wise. Either the advice-givers are not aligned with God's desire for you, or it's a projection of their fears and insecurities imposed on you. Fearing others' opinions is a dangerous trap of the enemy. Watch whose advice you take. Fearing people is a dangerous trap: "It is dangerous to be concerned with what others think of you, but if you trust the Lord, you are safe" (Proverbs 29:25 GNT).

**Type 2: Fear of being criticized by others.** Are you afraid of looking foolish in front of others? Stop focusing on what people think or might think of you. Remember the first man in Ruth chapter 4, who was next of kin to redeem the land that Naomi sold and also acquire Ruth? This was not Boaz who stepped up and became her kinsman redeemer. The man was a close relative who refused to be Ruth's redeemer because he did not want to jeopardize his inheritance by marrying a Moabitess. This man unknowingly rejected God's plans to make Ruth the great-grandmother of King David.

> *"The only one worthy of fear is God. "Do not be afraid of those who kill the body but cannot kill the soul. Rather, be afraid of the One who can destroy both soul and body in hell."*
> (Matthew 10:28 NIV)

Remember, *what can flesh do to you?* Even at such a young age, Jesus' fear and respect for God drove Him to prevent people from disrupting the temple. Jesus would rather have pleased God than man. Your goals can be accomplished by making bold moves like Jesus did at the temple.

**Type 3: Fear of other gods.** *Have you combined Christianity with idolatry?* Anything regarded above God can be considered an idol. *Are you enslaved to money?* No one can serve two masters. You have to pick one and despise the other (Matthew 6:24). *Are you afraid of what will happen if you let your idol go?* Try God, serve Him with all you've got, and watch Him do the impossible. "Do not worship any other gods or bow before them or serve them" (2 Kings 17:35 NIV). "Christ in you, [is] the hope of glory" (Colossians 1:27).

**Type 4: Fear of the unknown.** *Are you afraid of what the future holds? What is the "what if" in your life?* You do not want to embark on your dreams because you fear any adverse effects. *Do you know that every positive goal you have is orchestrated from above?* In Philippians 1:6 (NIV), "Being confident of this, that he who began a good work in you will carry it on to completion until the day of Christ Jesus." Do not allow fear to suffocate your dreams and goals. Do not fear the worst; let God take care of you and allow Him into your life. He is invested in you. God has "plans to prosper you and not to harm you, plans to give you hope and a future" (Jeremiah 29:11 NIV).

**Type 5: Fear of living.** *Are you paralyzed from living your life in fear of being rejected, not getting hired, not getting married, and not having kids or friends?* You may be worried that you are not where you ought to be compared to your peers. Afraid of whatever diseases or health conditions took your parents, family members, or friends? Your prosperity begins when you overcome those fears and start living with courage for the present moment and a bright future.

*"You cannot swim for new horizons
until you have courage to lose sight of the shore."*
—William Faulkner

**Type 6: Fear of failure.** The fear of failing is the most common. Failure is a growth pill if you can learn to swallow it and move on. It is the fear of committing a crime, making an error, or a mistake. There are lessons in failure. The list of inventors goes on about the people who tried numerous times and never gave up. Thomas Edison was one. He tried 1,000 times to generate electricity. His attitude about the failed attempts was phenomenal. He said, "I didn't fail 1,000 times. The light bulb was an invention with 1,000 steps." Remember the story of the Shunammite woman's dead son, Elisha, and Gehazi, Elisha's servant, in 2 Kings 4:18–37? Despite the prior demonstrative success, the staff failed to raise the boy until Elisha laid on him. Elisha had to change his strategy and did not give up after the first attempt.

**Type 7: Fear of solution.** The fear of solution is when you fear doing anything about your circumstance because of what the solution might bring or reveal. You are asking yourself, *"What if God does not intervene?"* The moment Peter began to doubt while walking on water, he began to sink. Jesus gave him a solution to have the courage to walk on water, but his faith wavered, and immediately he began to sink (Matthew 14:22–33).

**Type 8: Fear of rejection.** This fear makes you want to quit before even trying. Fear of rejection is that feeling you get when you do not apply for a job because you have already disqualified yourself. You are your worst critic. Approve yourself.

**Type 9: Fear of lack.** *Are you one of those who hoards every item for the possibility that they might need it someday?* That's a sign of fear of lack. Look inward to examine why you hold onto things, people, jobs, and relationships that no longer serve you. You have been told to let some of them go countless times, but you still hold on. Know that God will not withhold any good thing from you if you walk uprightly before Him. Psalm 84:1 (KJV) says, "For the Lord God is a sun and shield: the Lord will give grace and glory: no good thing will he withhold from them that walk uprightly."

**Type 10: Fear of success.** This fear is not knowing if you can handle the responsibility that comes with success. Identify why you fear success. Could it be that it would dominate your free time or your relationships?

**Type 11: Fear of death.** Are you constantly protecting your life and concerned that any action could result in death, to the point where you cannot live your life? You feel like you are living in bondage.

We must overcome fear to fulfill our purpose and reach our destiny.

### Seven Keys to Overcoming Fear

**1. Rebuke fear and make faith declarations.** Rebuke the spirit of fear and speak peace over every storm in your life, past or present. Be aware that God has already conquered every one of your storms before you ever get into one. Use the Word of God as your security blanket. Your daily assignment is to make declarations such as:

- I will not fear. I am no longer a slave to fear.
- I bind the spirit of fear.
- I am set free from all my fears
- I declare that the Spirit of supernatural love, power, a sound mind, and self-control live inside me.
- He that lives in me is greater than what I could ever encounter.
- I am an overcomer because Christ is my defender and conqueror.

**2. Realize the battle is not yours to fight.** When you go through tough times, believe that God is your firm foundation and that He will not leave you behind to suffer alone. God has won every battle and will not lose the battle over you. Understand that the Lord is still in the business of giving victories to His children (2 Chronicles 20:15, 17, 20). Do not fret. Fear is not the end of your journey. God did not bring you this far to leave you to fight your battles alone. He will get you to the next level, which is higher ground.

**3. Put your faith and trust in God.** Your victories are tied to your faith, not your worries or complaints. "And without faith, it is impossible to please God" (Hebrews 11:6 NIV). So, fix your eyes on the Author and Finisher of your faith, not on your circumstances (Hebrews 12:2). Faith in God allows you to move beyond worry and anxiety. Jesus calms the storm in Mark 4:35-41 (NIV). In verse 40, Jesus said, "Why are you afraid? Do you still have no faith?" We give the enemy access to our lives through fear and God access to our lives through faith. Faith pushes you forward toward your goals and destiny, while fear stagnates you in a position or moves you back to your past hurts and pains. So "commit everything you do to the Lord. Trust him, and he will help you" (Psalm 37:5 NKJV). God has not brought you this far to leave you. "Being confident of this, that he who began a good work in you will carry it on to completion until the day of Christ Jesus" (Philippians 1:6 NIV).

**4. Rejoice in the Lord; praise and worship Him.** Judah and Jerusalem's people rejoiced first before winning the battle (2 Chronicles 20:18, 21-22). They worshiped God even when they did not know the outcome. Always magnify the Lord. In Psalm 34, David said the Lord freed him from all his fears. David praised God through his fears, and he triumphed over his enemies. In the face of being sick, worship Him. In any circumstance, you find yourself, praise Him and give Him glory. Proclaim who He is. Say, "I have an almighty Father, and He is the King of Kings and the Lord of Lords, my goal redeemer."

> *"I prayed to the Lord, and he answered me.*
> *He freed me from all my fears.*
> *Those who look to him for help will be radiant with joy;*
> *no shadow of shame will darken their faces."*
> (Psalm 34:4-5 NLT)

**5. Remember past victories and proclaim the promises of God concerning you.** If you can remember all the battles that God enabled you to win, they should motivate you to hold onto God's Word concerning any circumstance you may pass through. The Judeans recounted what God did for the Israelites and were determined to stand with God regardless of what they faced, believing He would save them. Second Chronicles 20:6-9 (NIV) says, "Power and might are in your hand, and no one can withstand you. Our God, did you not drive out the inhabitants of this land before your people Israel and give it forever to the descendants of Abraham, your friend? They have lived in it and have built in it a sanctuary for your Name, saying, 'If calamity comes upon us, whether the sword of judgment, or plague or famine, we will stand in your presence before this temple that bears your Name and will cry out to you in our distress, and you will hear us and save us.'" We must remember the Lord "is able to do exceedingly abundantly above all that we ask or think, according to the power that works in us" (Ephesians 3:20 NKJV). In 1 John 4:4 (NIV), "You, dear children, are from God and have overcome them because the one who is in you is greater than the one who is in the world."

**6. Profess the Word.** "The Lord is on my side; I will not fear. What can man do to me?" (Psalm 118:6 ESV). Know the Scripture that counteracts your fears and proclaim it as often as possible. "For he will order his angels to protect you wherever you go" (Psalm 91:11-12 NLT). God promises to bring confidence and peace in the midst of the storm.

**7. Face your fears. Be bold and courageous.** You need to face your fears by walking with boldness. Take the limits off God. He can withstand every test you face. Stop restricting God. Be determined to overcome the devil's scheme and prevent him from having the last say. Let your attitude be that if God doesn't get me out of it, He will bless me through it. If you put too much emphasis on your fears, the devil will attack them. "For God has not given us a spirit of fear, but of power and of love and of a sound mind" (2 Timothy 1:7 NKJV). In other Bible translations, power is synonymous with courage, strength, and authority. In Deuteronomy 31:6, Moses urged the Israelites to be strong and courageous. He told them not to be afraid or panic, for God will personally go ahead of them, and He will not abandon them. In 1 Chronicles 28:20, David told Solomon the same thing—that God would be with him to finish the work of the temple. Risk everything on God; He will not let you fall without a net to catch you. Mark 11:23 (NLT) states, "I tell you the truth, you can say to this mountain, 'May you be lifted up and thrown into the sea,' and it will happen. But you must believe it will happen and have no doubt in your heart. You can pray for anything, and if you believe that you've received it, it will be yours."

Ultimately, fear is the feeling we get when we cannot control the outcome. Fear of things of men cannot coexist with fear of God. When you realize that you are never in control and God has all the control, you can finally surrender your life to Him. You need to surrender your pride and ego to God and let Him handle all the stuff (fear, doubts, and anxiety) that is out of control. Showers of blessings do not just happen—you have to make room for them. God wants to prepare you for His blessings. Make room for His showers to fall. And to do that, fear needs to stay out. Please continue to work on your fears until they have no control over you. Don't hesitate to seek professional assistance if necessary.

**Walk in Boldness**

> *"In whom we have boldness and access with*
> *confidence through our faith in him."*
> (Ephesians 3:12 ESV)

Setting goals and executing them takes courage and boldness. Often some tasks require more courage than others whereby you need audaciousness to reach an overarching goal. For instance, it could be acquiring an advocate position for a controversial topic, which may put you at risk of losing something important. Or it could be as risky as driving a long-distance interstate for the first time.

I remember the first time I drove three hundred miles across states. It took everything in me to summon the courage to do so. I had already been a driver in cities like New York City and Chicago for at least three years. I knew that the lifestyle I aspired to have would require the ability to embark on such activities to efficiently reach my goal of attending seminars and conferences on short notice. So, I had to make bold steps once and for all.

In my 1996 two-door coupe Toyota Paseo, I had my printed MapQuest directions (the navigating application before Google Maps), some CDs, drinks, and snacks prepared to enjoy my ride. I said my prayers, and off I went. On my way, whenever I would see an eighteen-wheeler, I would pray to God for the courage to drive past the trucks and not get crushed by any vehicle. During those moments, it felt like a lifetime journey. Then I would speed up just enough to pass them. As soon as I did, I would breathe out loud. I did this exercise for hours until I had mastered the strategy of not feeling like I would crash. The experience taught me how to face my fears head-on and overcome them with courage.

> *"Often in the real world, it is not the smart that get ahead but the BOLD."*
> –Robert Kiyosaki

So, what is boldness? According to the Oxford Dictionary, "boldness" is the willingness to take risks and act innovatively with confidence or courage. I define boldness as doing the right thing for your life despite the fears, doubts, and discomforts you feel. Being bold is critical to changing and growing to achieve your goals. It is a decision you make to reach your daily tasks.

I remember season three of the *American Idol* show in 2003. A contestant named William Hung boldly competed by singing one of Rick Martin's songs, "She Bangs." William wasn't close to being the best; in fact, his audition was rejected by the judges. However, his boldness to showcase his raw talent to millions of viewers landed him three record albums and other entertainment deals. Thus, being smart is good but not enough to get you ahead. It would be best if you made some bold moves. Do things you have never done before to get the results you have never had. Take the courage to learn something that may not be exciting but will surely get you ahead. Be willing to take calculated risks.

To walk in boldness, you should recognize what boldness is *not*. It is not poor planning or a lack of preparation. You shouldn't write an exam on the premise of being bold and not studying but expecting to pass. Boldness encompasses adequate preparation and planning. Hence, it is not abuse, rudeness, manipulation, or lording over people. Boldness should not be confused with any of those character flaws. Being rude is simply being rude. Hiding from challenges and avoiding necessary discussions are not characteristics of boldness.

You should cultivate the habit of addressing your challenges strategically. Having those difficult discussions enables you to handle situations efficiently. For instance, you may have a goal dependent on another person and can't understand why the work has not been done. Instead of avoiding that person or the matter, dare to have a planned discussion with prepared questions without casting judgment. This will get you the answers you need and allow you to continue your path to fulfilling your goal. Boldness does not also mean putting yourself down for the sake of humility. You need to take your stance without fear of appearing vulnerable.

To be bold, *what characteristics should you exhibit?* You need to put your trust and faith in God's strength. Realize that by your strength alone, you cannot prevail. Surrender your goals to God to guide you through each step of your plan while loving God and mankind.

A bold person is not afraid to be of service to God and others. Show compassion and express your heart in service. Call others to serve meaningfully and hold others accountable. Practice generosity by sowing today what you want to see tomorrow. Be bolder about your giving than about your getting or receiving.

Boldness takes courage and faith. It exudes confidence, humility, and self-awareness. Own your flaws and strengths gracefully. Don't tiptoe around your obstacles; have a plan and a process to address them. Taking bold steps without a plan is foolishness. Identify the things that are not working, draft a mechanism to tackle them, and execute it bravely. Boldly set healthy boundaries and do not indulge in fruitless activities or engage with people that drain you.

*What does the Bible say about boldness?* "For God has not given us a spirit of fear and timidity, but of power, love, and self-discipline" (2 Timothy 1:7 NLT). "The wicked flee, though no one pursues but the righteous are as bold as a lion" (Psalm 28:1 NIV). We know that a lion is brave, bold, and fearless. It is never timid or afraid, nor does it act cowardly when faced with oppositions. Boldness is a crucial ingredient for success in life and it must be centered on Christ. "Those who do wickedly against the covenant he shall corrupt with flattery, but the people who know their God shall be strong, and carry out great exploits" (Daniel 11:32 NKJV).

*What are you believing God to do in this season?* Does your goal need an ounce of boldness and courage to become a reality? Please know that God has given you what you need to sustain your race to the finish line. He wants you to live consciously and intentionally by taking bold steps. Everyone has the potential to win a race. Once the race starts, only those who are prepared for it win.

*Do you know God is committed to the seed He placed inside you?* If He put it inside of you, He has already given you all you need to nurture that seed to germination. The future of planting seeds is in its potential. Decide that you will accomplish so much this season that people will wonder if you had extra years to accomplish the tasks.

**Five Distinct Ways to Walk in Boldness**

**1. Employ the spirit of power.** *How do you get the spirit of power?* If you are a follower of Jesus Christ, you already have the spirit of power living inside of you. The Holy Spirit gives you the courage to make moves you could not have made logically. You become empowered to make bold, faith-filled declarations like "I can all do things through Christ who strengthens me." In Esther 4:16 (NIV), Esther summoned the courage to approach the king in an attempt to save her people from death. After she instructed her people to fast for three days, Esther said, "When this is done, I will go to the king, even though it is against the law. And if I perish, I perish."

The spirit of power gives you the confidence to face your fears and conquer them. You will have the strength to bear the unbearable if you rely on the spirit of power within you. According to Ephesians 3:20, the spirit of power is at work within every believer to do exceedingly abundantly above all that we can ask or think. Know that powerlessness is victimization by the enemy. Lack of power will keep you fearful and hold you hostage from reaching your full potential. Decide to tap into your inner strength centered on Christ. If you do not know how to do it, seek professional and spiritual assistance.

**2. Embrace God's love.** Walking in boldness requires having confidence in God's love for you. You must remember that God is committed to you. His love has no bounds. God wants to give you more than you can ever think or imagine. The book of Daniel 11:32 explains that spiritually mature people will be strong and do exploits. The Scripture mentions being strong, showing strength, and standing firm before doing great exploits or acting. If you can rest in God's love, the reflection, awareness, and consciousness of His love will erode fear. Fear is bound to occur and rule out boldness where there is no love. Embracing God's love includes loving others and ourselves. Love for others allows us to indulge and focus on bold service. Love for yourself should drive you to boldly establish healthy boundaries when others want to take advantage of or abuse you. Note that the keywords I used are "want to." If you teach people how to treat you, this should prevent others from abusing you. Nevertheless, you cannot control what others do but what you allow them to do to you.

**3. Have a sound mind.** Before you can walk in boldness, your mind must be set to the right frequency. Meaning you must have the mental capacity to make rational decisions. This demands that you make decisions to think positively about your goals. I have written a whole chapter on authority over your thoughts. Positive thinking can quiet your fears. You must win the battle in your mind saying that you can't do this or that. If you let your mind drift in multiple directions, it will give you multiple reasons why you should not tackle a task or make a bold decision. So, train your mind to manifest your desires and then act. Imagine what your positive mindset will look and feel like when that goal comes to fruition.

**4. Acknowledge past victories.** Let your past victories fuel your boldness to face any circumstances. Don't let your boldness be out of ego or a need to exert control, but let it be out of humility before the power of the higher one. Don't be like Goliath, who used his size and fear to oppress people. Remember every lion and bear that you have defeated. Be grateful for the past lessons you learned, too. Focus on what the Lord has already done. Leave what has not happened to Him. Quit focusing on how but rather on *who*, and lean not on your understanding.

You will never know what's on the other side of the door if you don't make a move. If, for some reason, you cannot find the keys to the door ahead of you, simply turn back to the open doors behind you and glorify God for His kindness and all your wins.

**5. Purge every guilt.** Don't allow guilt and sin to sabotage your boldness. Your past sins and unrighteousness want to guilt-trip you and keep you from walking in boldness. Refuse to succumb to every lie and deceit waging war on you. Repent of your sin. And be confident that you are forgiven. Do the necessary work to get yourself out of guilt and sin. Do not give life to your past failures. Your future is more valuable and powerful than your past. Remember that you already have the ability to give birth to your future.

Boldness involves understanding your strengths and weaknesses and then moving beyond them. Don't try to hide your imperfections, problems, or failures. Accept them as part of you. This will allow you to move forward confidently while rising above them. You need to appreciate your uniqueness and devise means to overcome your weaknesses. God is more powerful than your giants—be bold!

> *"Don't focus on the size of your problem.*
> *Focus on the size of your God."*
> –Pastor Tony Evans

---

**Moving Forward**

**Self-determination:** Do something about your fear. Decide to rise and not run from your fears. Be determined to break free of your past and fight every appearance of fear. Identify your fears and tackle them using God's principles. You need to walk with God. Meditate on Psalm 23 and Psalm 27:1-2. Remember, the devil's agenda is to kill, steal, and destroy (John 10:10). He wants to use fear to keep you from achieving your God-given goals. Be alert and watchful of the enemy's scheme. Write down your top two dimensions of fear and state a deliberate act you will take to counter each area.

**Embody God's love, boldness, and self-control:** Envelop yourself in God's love with a sound mind, self-discipline, sound judgment, and sobriety. Where there is agape, fear cannot live. One of the reasons people struggle with fear is that they don't know the love of God as well as they should. "Eye has not seen, nor ear heard, Nor have entered into the heart of man. The things which God has prepared for those who love Him" (1 Corinthians 2:9 NKJV). Let God's unconditional love give you the courage to confront your fears. "Perfect love casts out fear" (1 John 4:18 NKJV). As Bishop T. D. Jakes said, when you face storms in life, let your "boat" float, as long as you don't let the situation on the outside get on the inside.

Waterproof your boat by affirming God's Word. There is power in the tongue. Memorize Scriptures that profess boldness and courage. Have faith to walk on your water to Jesus, keeping your gaze fixed on Him.

**Consistently lift your protective shield of faith:** Extinguish all the flaming arrows of your fear in every circumstance. Decide to defeat fear daily by taking your first steps. Think of a staircase and summon the courage to make progress by taking one step at a time. And try it again the next day. Declare that your faith will push you forward whenever fear appears. Whenever the spirit of fear wants to rise, deliberately make a bold move even though you are scared.

**Prayer points:** Add the points below to your prayer list.

- Lord, empower me to cast away every form of fear holding me back from pursuing your plans for my life.
- Lord, paralyze every spirit that causes me to fear.
- I break every stronghold and the fear of falsehoods in my life. I bind and cast out the spirit of fear now and forever.
- I pray against the voice of fear, which are lies of the enemy to be silenced.
- I pray that the voice of Truth fills my mind and that I will be strong and do exploits.
- I pray for the spirit of supernatural boldness to fill me.

**Praise and worship God through your "storm."** I define praise as a declaration of who God is and a means to offer gratitude for what He has done, while worship is to revere God's glory with your body, soul, and spirit. Find songs that resonate with you and your situation. Here are some of my favorite songs:

- Tasha Cobbs Leonard ("Overflow," "Break Every Chain," and "Fill Me Up")
- Travis Greene ("Made a Way" and "Soul will Sing")
- VaShawn Mitchell ("Nobody Greater")
- Steve Crown ("All the Glory," "You are Great," and "We Wait on You")
- Sonnie Badu ("Covenant Keeping God," "Let it Rain," and "Baba")
- Hezekiah Walker ("Amazing," "I Need you To Survive," and "God Favored Me")
- Anthony Brown ("Trust in You," "Miracle," and "Worth") Miranda Curtis ("The Lord's Song" and "Nobody Like You") Rita Springer ("Worth It All")
- CeCe Winans ("Goodness of God" and "Alabaster Box"), and artists alike.

From Elevation Worship and Maverick City Music, I treasure the following worship songs: "Never lost a battle," "Rattle," "Firm Foundation," "See A Victory," "Surrounded (Fight my battles)," "Jireh," "Promises," "Same God," and "Do It Again." From Hillsong Worship, my favorite songs are "So Will I (100 Billion X)," "Broken Vessels," "What a Beautiful Name," and "Spirit Lead Me." The Famous For (I Believe) song by Tauren Wells and Jenn Johnson is one of my family's favorites.

Meditate on the lyrics of the song that resonate with your spirit. Listen to them countless times as you go through your day. Below are the lyrics to one of my favorite songs by Osinachi "Sinach" Okoro, titled "I Know Who I Am." I sing and dance to this song during good and challenging times. I won't stop dancing until I feel liberated and have peace. This song declares who I am in Christ and the power within me.

"We are a chosen generation
We've been called forth to show His excellence
All I require for life, God has given me
And I know who I am

I know whom God says I am
What He says I am
Where He says I'm at
I know who I am

I'm walking in power,
I'm working miracles
I live a life of favor,
For I know who I am

Oh oh oh, oh oh oh
I know who I am

I am holy,
I am righteous oh . . .
I am so rich,
I am beautiful

> I'm walking in power,
> I'm working miracles
> I live a life of favor,
> For I know who I am
>
> Take a look at me. I'm a wonder
> It doesn't matter what you see now
>
> Can you see His glory?
> For I know who I am
>
> Oh oh oh, oh oh oh
> I know who I am."

**Position yourself for holy boldness:** Do the work! Be ready. Like Isaiah 6 says, "Here I am, send me!" Joshua positioned himself for the battle, and he never lost. "Be not afraid or discouraged. For the LORD your God is with you wherever you go" (Joshua 1:9 NLT). Seek assistance if needed. Paul asked the church to pray for him to preach the gospel with courage.

**Plan to take bold steps:** Complete tangible tasks to gain victory. Make a list of areas where you need boldness. Start by being honest about what holds you back. What have you not accomplished because it's just uncomfortable? What task or conversation makes you cringe when you think about it? What goal has been haunting you for years? *What do you regularly procrastinate on because it's not fun?* It is important to identify these opportunities by writing them down, big or small. Make a list. It won't be pretty, but it's necessary. Just get it all out. Start with a small battle you think you can win, map out a plan, and take the field. Winning builds confidence as well as your reputation.

**Make bold moves:** Create bold goals and act toward them. You need to have bold faith in your goals. Pray bold prayers, asking for the desires of your heart, declaring exactly how you want to achieve your goals and when. Ask for bold breakthroughs. Write and make bold affirmations about your goals. Recite them daily, both before you start your day and during it. Make magnificently bold declarations concerning your goals and declare that the past season will be the lowest you will have been in your life, marriage, business, or career. Sing and rejoice with bold praise and worship. Have bold expectations. Act boldly, like someone who is already walking in victory. Serve boldly without being ashamed or worried about what others think. When fear knocks on your door, open the door with faith.

**Take risks:** The greatest risk is taking no risks. Take calculated risks. Examine whether the results outweigh possible losses from taking the risk. There can only be two outcomes. It's either a yes or a no. Take the chance to get a yes, and if you don't receive it, then trust that you will learn from the failure, gain resiliency, or, better yet, trust that a better and more significant opportunity will come your way.

**Seek knowledge:** Increase your knowledge in the area you are afraid of to gain the courage and confidence to overcome your fear. Seek resources, apply reputable strategies, and empower yourself with knowledge. Be consistent in studying relevant materials regularly.

CHAPTER 7

# Principle 5
# Develop Patience and Perseverance

*"But if we look forward to something we don't yet have, we must wait patiently and confidently."* (Romans 8:25 NLT)

A flashback to the first house I purchased in the Midwest depicts one of my manifestations of impatience. I had gotten a job in a different state and had little time to get the house ready for sale, so I decided to rent the property. Boy, was I impatient to get a renter. I quickly rented the property to a family without a thorough background check, and the tenant defaulted on my rental fees from the second month they moved in. It was an uphill battle to get the court to get them out after living for three months for free. I thought I had learned my lesson, so for the next tenant, I did a thorough background check that revealed the applicant had lied about having a job. But since I did not have any other interested applicants and the one at hand had given me a sob story about the job situation, I rented it out. Not surprisingly, I experienced the same thing, and no payment was received after the move-in rent. I was devastated, so I made a short sale on the house. Impatience will cost you.

*Why does your goal seem to be taking forever to be realized?* When you have done it all—read all the self-help and goal-setting books; known how to set a SMART goal; and taken care of your internal and external interference—sometimes all you have left to do is have patience.

Although you might be good at setting goals, some of your goals might not be accomplishable within your desired time frame. Other goals might take time before they can be realized. *How do you manage such goals? What do you do during the waiting season?* The story of prophet Elisha and the Shunammite woman in the Bible reminds us that all hope is not lost with our goals, even if we have biological or physical limitations. The Shunammite woman could not fathom having a baby with her husband in old age. She gave birth to a son within a year of Elisha's prophecy. Her hospitality to Elisha, which included providing him a chamber to stay in whenever he was in town, prompted her blessing. Then one day, Elisha thought to bless her with her heart's desires.

> *"The secret of patience is to do something else in the meantime."*
> –Croft M. Pentz

Croft Pentz's quote states that the "something else" you do in your waiting season is crucial to the results you get. I heard of a testimony in England where a couple had been looking for the fruit of the womb for fourteen years. Medically, they were told by different physicians that they could never have a child. Throughout their waiting season, the husband would lay hands on his wife and declare that she would get pregnant, and they would have children. Faithfully, after fourteen years, they had a baby girl and named her Evidence. The Word of God in Isaiah 40:31 states, "But they who wait for the Lord shall renew their strength; they shall mount up with wings like eagles; they shall run and not be weary; they shall walk and not faint." God is a master economist; He never wastes any of our experiences. He would use your waiting period to renew your strength and give you the power to fight your battles. God wants to prepare you for your harvest season. That's when you receive answers to your prayers in a manner you cannot think of or imagine. *Do you confidently trust in God's plans for your life? Can you lay down your heavy burdens at the Lord's feet?*

Please do not mistake your waiting period as: God has forgotten you or thinks you misunderstood your purpose. Your destination is still there, calling for you to move toward it. Each step in the direction God leads will get you to that glorious destination. Do the work during your waiting period, and don't get frustrated. God will lay the work on your heart that needs to be done. Your wait is your time to serve, worship, discover, grow, develop, and acquire a new toolset for the journey ahead to an expected end. Get lost in service like the Shunamite woman and trust in His promise like Abraham. The Lord told Abraham He would bring the Israelites to a land flowing with milk and honey. And He did after a long period. God never reneges on his promise. Winning the battle requires holding on a little longer. God is working it out.

> *"To lose patience is to lose the battle."*
> –Mahatma Gandhi

You do not want to quit in your waiting period and miss what God has prepared for you in your later seasons. You cannot fulfill all righteousness until you know what God has placed inside you. Ask God for what He has deposited inside of you. With God, there is an agenda for every experience we go through. To fulfill that agenda, we must know who we are in Christ, our seed for greatness.

*What's inside of you?* It took Jesus years to increase in wisdom and stature before He would begin His ministry. He then knew exactly what to say in different circumstances to heal people. Jesus knew in what situation He needed to stoop down and wash His disciples' feet. *How in sync are you with what God has deposited in you?*

Patience is an act and a practice of being resolute amid expectations without erupting into angst. It's one of the fruits of the Spirit that builds our perseverance and endurance. It's a key to building hope and faith—knowing that your goal will be achieved without depending on time.

Studies have shown that patience stems from one's childhood and how the child was nurtured. Gradually, whatever we learned morphed into adulthood, and our interactions with others established our patience level. Outside of the necessities, as a child, I barely got what I wanted regarding clothes, snacks, or vacations. So, I bought myself everything I wanted when I became an adult. Most times, I acted hastily, afraid that if I didn't decide quickly, I would forever lose the opportunity to acquire them. I did not know that I was exhibiting a low level of patience.

On the other hand, other people might experience a different childhood, where they receive everything they want quickly. But that experience taught them to receive with immediate effect, which could lead to a lack of patience. Understand your source of patience or lack of it. Learning your triggers is one of the keys to leading a successful life and accomplishing your goals.

Identifying what triggers your impatience will help you manage your goals. This trigger is different for everyone. For some, it might be their environment, food, other people's behavior, or choice of words. I encourage you to study your mood and take note of your triggers for a month. Note what external factors change your feelings or mood from patience to impatience. What were the warning signs of your impatience? These signs will help you recognize when to manage your feelings and consciously practice patience.

Whenever I am experiencing a moment of impatience, my whole body becomes restless, and I start to jiggle my legs and pace up and down; I cannot sit still and begin to breathe faster. All these signs do not come at once. The jiggling of legs is the first sign. It escalates to fast breathing if not controlled, and other signs follow. Then I face the consequences of making rushed decisions. I had gone through these situations numerous times before I learned my lesson. Although I wrote this whole book in a few weeks, I consistently had to relax and take deep breaths to stop myself from publishing it immediately. I consciously restrained myself and took time to edit, get beta readers, and solicit feedback before publishing it for at least six months after writing. I had already accomplished my goal of writing a book, but to effectively impact people with it, I had to take time to polish the content through multiple edits.

When you are patient, God will lift you out of your despair and solidify your stance so that you will rejoice and testify to His doings so that others can trust Him. "I waited patiently for the LORD; he turned to me and heard my cry. He lifted me out of the slimy pit, out of the mud and mire; he set my feet on a rock and gave me a firm place to stand. He put a new song in my mouth, a hymn of praise to our God. Many will see and fear the LORD and put their trust in him" (Psalm 40:1–3 NIV).

Impatience breeds frustration, unhappiness, stress, irritability, anxiety, and anger. If you let go of a situation and do not lose patience or even react negatively, you are in control. Contrary opinions may regard that situation as powerless or weak. But we can act logically and perform better when we can control our emotions and actions without reacting hurriedly. Controlled situations lead to productive outcomes.

Getting stuck in traffic is where you see impatient people losing control and blurting out foul language. Often, their behaviors do not produce a positive result but rather anger, frustration, and road rage. A lack of patience can ruin and rob you of your life's goals and success.

Honestly, impatience is an excuse to fail. Losing patience quickly means a lack of self-control, which causes people not to want to be around you or work with you. It affects your relationships with your children, siblings, friends at home, work, and everywhere else, and your marriage. While some people naturally have the gift of patience, others do not. But it is a skill that can be learned.

*"The key to everything is patience.*
*You get the chicken by hatching the egg,*
*not by smashing it open."*
–Arnold Glasow, American humorist

Patience is required in different areas of our lives. To succeed, you must be patient with yourself, family members, co-workers, peers, the church, the government, strangers, your circumstances, and God. Patience with yourself is extending grace to yourself, not being hard on your failures, or being in a hurry to make decisions. Self-patience is perseverance through the time it takes to reach your goals in finding your desired job, getting promoted, making a purchase, losing weight, or any prolonged time-dependent task.

Patience with yourself will require determination, focus, and motivation to follow through on the journey to your goal post. It takes practicing patience to expand your territory of abundance, even when you face frustrating circumstances and unpleasant situations.

Ephesians 4:2 tells us to "be completely humble and gentle; be patient, bearing with one another in love." Patience with others transforms relationships. It is essential because your goals are connected to others, more than likely. Having patience helps you not make rash relationship decisions or be misunderstood. Mind you, having patience with others does not indicate weakness but love.

As Ephesians 4:2 says, we should bear with one another in love. Love is patient and kind. If accomplishing your goals requires others to complete a task, you should strive to practice patience like others have been patient with you. Though this might be challenging, understanding their limitations and giving people the benefit of the doubt helps. Note that while you have empathy, you must choose your words and behaviors carefully so they do not negatively impact the situation's outcome.

The circumstances you encounter can test your patience, especially if you have no power over the outcome. For example, it could be that you are impatient with starting a family, meeting your life partner, seeking child support, or processing a lawsuit. It could also be as basic as putting the kids to bed, dealing with rude people, or getting stuck in traffic.

Whatever the circumstance, the ability to remain calm is a virtue. Thank God I have learned how to react to challenging situations, hold my peace, and remain calm in dire situations. And I tell you, it is a new freedom when practicing patience.

In addition to freedom, there are other benefits to being patient. Schnitker research studies reported that people with increased interpersonal patience exhibited decreased depression, higher goal achievement, and enhanced well-being. Patient people suffer fewer stress-related illnesses and tend to live healthy lifestyles. They are considered good decision-makers, productive, and team players at their workplaces.

In Job 42, Job remained patient with God when Satan conducted an experiment to test him by taking away his possessions. Even when Job's health was affected, he never cursed God. He kept praying through his circumstances, which he might have perceived as a fleeting life.

God rewarded Job's perseverance at the end of the temptation by restoring what he had lost with more than he could have thought or imagined. I challenge you to walk with God as you go through your life's troubles and watch how He transforms them. Patience strengthens your faith and builds your inner core and capacity to face and overcome challenges.

I firmly believe in the verse that says "everything is possible for the one who believes" (Mark 9:23 CSB). Patience can cure and solve a variety of problems. An African proverb says, "Patience can cook a stone," meaning that you can solve complex problems with lots of patience.

> *"Be still before the LORD and wait patiently for him; do not fret when people succeed in their ways, when they carry out their wicked schemes. Refrain from anger and turn from wrath; do not fret—it leads only to evil. For those who are evil will be destroyed, but those who hope in the LORD will inherit the land."*
> (Psalm 37:7-9 NIV)

Psalm 37:7-9 teaches us to rest, be silent, trust in the Lord, and not be bothered when others indulge in unjust things to achieve success. However, it finishes off in verse 9, insinuating that you will receive a reward for your waiting, meaning that your delay is neither denial nor rejection.

Remain still, unmovable, and hopeful in your waiting period, knowing there is a gain in having patience.

Here are some ways to practice patience if this is not one of your supernatural gifts:

**Keys to Exercising Patience**

**1. Embrace your season of waiting.** *How do you act while you wait?* Your waiting season is an opportunity to cultivate an attitude of gratitude. Practice thanksgiving while you anticipate what God has in store for you. This is not the time to start complaining, becoming fretful, or grumbling about what hasn't happened. This will only fuel frustration, bitterness, and anger if you entertain it. Instead, spend time appreciating the little things and serving. Use the time to focus on helping others achieve their goals. Please do not take your wait, which is your pruning season, for granted. Utilize the opportunity to prune yourself from things that might hinder you from reaching your goals. When I was seeking to get married, I served brides during their wedding plans and ceremonies wherever they needed assistance. I did not care if they were younger or my mentees. My service at weddings was an appreciation of God's blessings in their lives and a way to attract the same thing in my life. God was building my humility, and others who noticed extended similar favors. I remember people who provided tremendous service on my wedding day at no cost. Use your waiting season wisely to build character and grow in the fruits of the Spirit, such as joy, peace, kindness, love, patience, faithfulness, goodness, gentleness, and self-control. Thank God through your waiting season.

2. **Know your triggers.** Learn what aggravates you and strategize a way to manage it. For some, it might be talking to certain people, eating certain foods, being in a particular environment, or engaging in online activities. Know what triggers your short- or long-term impatience and devise a strategy to eliminate it. Mine is Facebook. I intentionally stay passive in my usage because sometimes, things are posted that make me impatient about my goals or unhappy with my progress. Besides blocking people or silencing notifications, I cannot control any of the activities posted by friends and family. However, I use TikTok and YouTube because I have some control over what slides into my feeds. Suppose inappropriate messages happen to fall through. I can either flag or report them. It is critical to identify your triggers and counteract them.

3. **Use a stress-relief valve.** Acquire a tool or action that helps you relieve tension to control your impatience, like keeping a motivational stress ball handy to help you focus and remain grounded. Or you could use drinking hot tea, journaling, body relaxation techniques, dancing, singing, meditation, or praying. If you cannot control your feelings, you can choose appropriate behaviors to manage your emotions. Take a time-out for a short period to slow down your heart rate but feel free to extend the time until you feel calm and settled. Practice taking deep and slow breaths whenever you start to feel impatient. My go-to stress relief valve is to use my thoughts to control my emotions. To induce a positive thought and change my mood, I look at my screensaver on my phone since it's a photo of my vision board. When I start feeling impatient, the images on my board remind me of my life's direction and help me focus on my goals instantly. Find a healthy stress reliever and implement it.

**4. Adjust your expectations.** You cannot control people and their situations, so learn to adjust your expectations, expect disruptions, and allow open perspectives when dealing with others. Adjustments do not mean expecting the worst from people or accepting foolishness. But instead, show empathy, have compassion, and extend grace to others. Learn to put things in perspective. For example, *what if you were the cause of a delay? How would you want the offended to treat you?* In dealing with difficult people, you will be required to choose the right words and actions that will keep you calm so you do not lose your patience or even theirs. Constantly adjust your expectations and apply humor as necessary. You cannot hold people to high standards, set high expectations, and not expect them to disappoint you. Leave room for failure. Even children whose parents have a positive influence and expect the children to act accordingly often let them down. So how much more will your acquaintances or associates let you down? Therefore, accept the laws of human nature and extend grace.

**5. Submit it to God.** Being patient requires faith and trust in God. Psalm 37:5 (KJV) says, "Commit thy ways unto the Lord, trust also in him, and he shall bring it to pass." Patience is believing that God will fulfill all your goals in His time. Submission is not trying to circumvent the situation like Sarah did with Abraham. Sarah impatiently gave her maid to her husband so that he could have a child, even after the Lord had told them they would have a child together. Patience is not indulging in activities that try to rush God through covenants and oaths. God's arms are not too short to save, nor His ears too dull to hear (Isaiah 59:1). There is no need to keep reminding God of your goals every day and moment. Be sure to add to your list of affirmations that you will wait on the Lord's will.

**6. Ask for support.** Don't be afraid to ask others for help. Delegate tasks that others can complete or hire someone to do them. In general, ask God to support you on your journey to acquiring the skill of patience. Galatians 5:22-25 (AMP) reveals that patience is a fruit of the Spirit, and the Holy Spirit empowers our conduct. Each day when you get up, ask the Holy Spirit to empower your inner spirit to conduct yourself with self-control and discipline. Romans 12:12 (AMP) says, "constantly rejoicing in hope [because of our confidence in Christ], steadfast and patient in distress, devoted to prayer [continually seeking wisdom, guidance, and strength]."

*"A man who is a master of patience is a master of everything else."*
–George Saville

Recognize that there are things in life that you have no power over. It takes patience and the grace of God to accomplish anything in life. You may have the power to control your thoughts and manage your feelings and actions, but everything else is out of your control. Be patient with yourself, others, and your circumstances until it becomes a habit.

---

**Moving Forward**

**Season of waiting:** Even if your season of waiting might seem too long to achieve your desires, please use this time efficiently. Get busy with gratitude and pour your life into the matters and affairs that will help counter impatience. Give Him praise while you are at it. This season is an opportunity for you to grow and eliminate any unrighteous entanglements. Please don't waste your waiting period complaining or being frustrated. Pray through your season without ceasing.

**Self-discipline:** You must exercise self-control to keep to your goals. Know your triggers and work on counteracting each one that leads to the feeling of impatience. Let your behavior, words, and thoughts align with waiting patiently. Discipline your thoughts so that they can control your feelings toward being patient. Whenever you start to feel impatient, resist making hasty decisions. Develop a strategy to help manage your impatience if you have to go on time-out, meditate, or take deep breaths, and do so to calm your mind and body.

**Expectations:** If you expect others to act according to your standards, stop it. People have different values and follow various codes of conduct based on their religion, culture, and environment; thus, always leave room for differences. Show compassion and extend grace to others.

**Support**: Seek support from people to take you off the edge. Most importantly, ask the Lord to give you the spirit of patience and the grace to wait.

CHAPTER 8

# Principle 6
# Have Authority Over Your Thoughts

*"A man's mind plans his way as he journeys through life,
But the Lord directs his steps and establishes them."*
(Proverbs 16:9 AMP)

It would be outrageous to say that I have always had authority over my thoughts. I am one of those people who can have a thousand thoughts in a few seconds. You could be having a conversation with me, and the next minute I may blurt out a sentence totally irrelevant to our discussion topic. My thoughts tend to race so quickly and bounce around at times. I know there is a medical condition for this, but I am yet to get tested. It's called attention deficit disorder (ADD). Let's assume I am a functioning, undiagnosed ADD adult who has learned coping skills for programming my mind to attract what I want. I can attest that it works. Working on controlling your mind is one of the keys to living successfully and accomplishing your desires.

*Do you have the mindset to be blessed? How important is what we think? Does it matter?* One of my favorite quotes, Proverbs 23:7 (KJV) says, "As a man thinketh in his heart, so he is." *Do you know you can co-create what you desire through conscious thoughts?* You feed your subconscious mind with your desired outcomes by deliberately thinking positively. Infuse your environment with positive self-talk and godly thoughts, and watch the light of God in your life radiate. *Have you ever met people who are always positive, even in dire situations?* Some of them have it figured out. They have identified a core belief system that cannot be shaken. To reach your goals, you must stop all self-limiting thoughts and substitute purposeful ones for them. Eliminate negative thoughts by applying strong emotions to feed and dominate your life. You cannot give birth to what you are not impregnated with. "Now to Him who is able to do far more abundantly beyond all that we ask or think according to the power that works within us" (Ephesians 3:20 ESV). Take captive of your thoughts and yield them to Christ. "Casting down imaginations, and every high thing that exalteth itself against the knowledge of God, and bringing into captivity every thought to the obedience of Christ" (2 Corinthians 10:5 KJV).

> *"Finally, believers, whatever is true, whatever is honorable and worthy of respect, whatever is right and confirmed by God's word, whatever is pure and wholesome, whatever is lovely and brings peace, whatever is admirable and of good repute; if there is any excellence, if there is anything worthy of praise, think continually on these things [center your mind on them, and implant them in your heart]."*
> (Philippians 4:8 AMP)

The mind is the interface between your body and spirit. Many people are victims of the content of their minds. Are you a victim of wrong thinking? Disengagement from the spirit of wrongful thought must first occur to release you from that mindset before reconfiguration can follow. Restructure your mind to align with thoughts of good.

## Understanding the Mind

Your mind controls a physical brain. At the same time, the unseeable mind houses all imaginations, beliefs, and thoughts. It is the part of humans that engages in conscious thinking and decision-making. The intelligence of your mind permeates every cell of your body, not just brain cells. Your mind has tremendous power over all bodily systems. The mind continuously assimilates, processes, recognizes, and evaluates information. It not only gathers experience and knowledge but also controls how you view yourself and perceive the world.

When a thought comes to us, the mind processes the information, discards it, hangs onto it for further evaluation, or saves it in memory. The mind never rests, even while we sleep. It continuously works to process information or might even unconsciously engage in a solution activity and appear in your dreams as visions or nightmares.

> *"The vision that you glorify in your mind, the ideal that you enthrone in your heart—this you will build your life by, and this you will become."*
> –James Lane Allen

The mind is powerful. It affects your bodily function. It is said that the mind causes eighty percent of illnesses. Have you had ulcers from worrying or gotten sick from viewing a horrific video or image on TV? It could even be that you had weak knees after hearing bad news. Thoughts cause all these symptoms. Likewise, the mind affects behavior. What is in your mind comes to the surface and influences your behavior. If your mind is filled with love and kindness, it would be natural to be loving and kind. On the other hand, if your mind is filled with anger and hatred, you would be more predisposed to demonstrate angry and hateful behavior.

In addition, the mind produces energy. The mind can set things in motion to create. For example, an architect draws a plan to create a blueprint before any developer can start building a house. Scientific inventions like airplanes, turbines, and engines were first created in the mind. The mind's power plays a significant role in sports such as golf and tennis. Superhuman power is often seen in times of crisis. In 2009, a man in Kansas lifted a heavy Mercury sedan off a six-year-old girl trapped underneath when it backed out on top of her. He must have been able to conceive the action in his mind before attempting it physically.

Also, adrenaline is released into your bloodstream in a crisis, giving you enormous energy for extraordinary action. In the first-year engineering design class that I teach, I start the class by telling my students to look around their environment and call out what they see. They mention technology, furniture, physical space, software, and structures. All these were conceived in a man's mind before they were built. And they need to permit their minds to explore. Do you know you are one thought away from your next novel product or service? A man's creativity, ideas, and innovation are hidden in his mind. The first stage of achieving your goals is in your mind.

In the Bible, do you know that the mind is analogous to the heart, not the brain? Romans 7:23 (NLT) emphasizes the law of one's mind: ". . . that is at war with my mind," indicating that the mind is a battleground. Please keep in mind that the battleground is a spiritual one rather than a geographical or physical one. Spiritual forces and mental forces affect the physical world. There is a constant battle in your mind to please God or sin. We serve the Lord with our minds; therefore, the mind is a precious resource to access. So, there is a spiritual battle we engage in every day.

Various forces are at work seeking to take control of our minds, whether we like it or not. The devil, the world, and our sinful nature conspire to take our minds captive. "For our struggle is not against flesh and blood, but against the rulers, against the powers, against the world forces of this darkness, against the spiritual forces of wickedness in the heavenly places" (Ephesians 6:12 NIV). We need to be alert and of sober mind (1 Peter 5:8) to prepare for the battleground.

The mind affects our being and behavior. If we lose the fight in our minds, we might as well forget winning physically. What's in your mind comes to the surface in how you express yourself. You will quickly act out those virtues if your mind is filled with joy, love, peace, and kindness. Likewise, the opposite is also true. If your mind is filled with hatred, anger, and discouragement, you will act them out. If positive words are sown in your mind consistently, it will be natural for you to lead a triumphant life. What's inside your mind will eventually come out. So, a sound mind becomes the bedrock of a healthy, fruitful, and victorious life.

A new mind means a new perception of how you look at your circumstances. Perception has everything to do with your progress. You cannot step into your future and stay stuck in your old mindset. A new life requires a new mind. Have you heard of the saying that you cannot use old thoughts to yield new solutions? With the knowledge of the mind's spiritual anatomy, you can bring your goals into existence with the architecture and content of your mind. "Be careful how you think; your life is shaped by your thoughts" (Proverbs 4:23 GNT). The NCV version states, "Be careful what you think, because your thoughts run your life," while the NRSV translation says, "Flow the spring of life."

Our thoughts fuel our actions. Do you know that your identity is a function of your mind? Our thoughts become realities. So, it is fair to say that where you are today has much to do with your thinking. Do you believe your SMART goal can still be accomplished this year alone? Can your mind conceive this? *What are your self-limiting beliefs? Are you telling yourself I am not smart, no one would love me, and I can never get out of debt?* You might be required to debunk some myths and self-limiting beliefs, such as *"They would never hire a person like me," "No one in my family has been able to achieve such a goal in their lifetime,"* or *"Who am I to want more than the status quo?"* My life story is a testament that God can do the impossible. Trust that God is still in the business of giving you your heart's desires (Psalm 37:4).

**Mindsets to Avoid**

There are thoughts you should avoid at all costs to reach your goals. Your thoughts can change the trajectory of your life. They can either drag you down or build you up. If you think wrong, you can go wrong. Since the mind is a bedrock, take authority over these mindsets below.

**Victim Mind:** *What is a victim mindset?* You are a victim of your circumstance. Your past experiences may have scared you so much that you have built a bulletproof, protective mindset that nothing good or evil can penetrate. You may have trouble taking responsibility for your life and blame others for what you are experiencing, especially when you believe you had nothing to do with your past failures. Living as a victim may give the impression that you believe the enemy or have few opportunities to grow. This mindset leaves no room for love, hope, joy, and faith to operate fully in your life. Looking from the outside in, it seems the victim mindset enjoys the position; however, one of the enemy's schemes allows people to barricade themselves behind such a mindset. The healing process starts when you recognize that you have this mindset and begin to renounce it. As believers, "overwhelming victory is ours through Christ, who loved us" (Romans 8:37 NLT).

**Anxious Mind**: Anxious thoughts are driven by anxiety or fear, leading to irrational thoughts, delusion, or even mental conditions like paranoia if not treated. If you are constantly afraid that someone is out to get you or feel suffocated by something, you may have developed paranoia and should seek help. The anxious mindset I'm referring to here is the mind that is dominated by or acts on worry. An anxious mind is consumed by people's feelings about you and their perception of your actions. When you give in to anxiety, you become worried, which leads to unfruitfulness. "Can all your worries add a single moment to your life?" (Luke 12:25 NLT). A worried mind leads to defeat. You can't win in the physical realm if your mind is already defeated. Notice that God created spectacular things by speaking His Word. Being purposeful about where you plant the Word is critical. "The worries of this life and the deceitfulness of wealth choke the word, making it unfruitful" (Matthew 13:22 NIV). Surrender your thoughts to God to move away from anxious and worrisome thoughts. "Do not be anxious about anything, but in every situation, by prayer and petition, with thanksgiving, present your requests to God. And the peace of God, which transcends all understanding, will guard your hearts and your minds in Christ Jesus" (Philippians 4:6-7 NIV).

**Doubtful Mind**: A person with a doubtful mind struggles with believing in herself, her family, other people, the government, and even the voice of the Lord. You still doubt the possible outcome when you are presented with factual evidence. The antidote to doubt is belief. The Bible says in Mark 11:24 (NIV), "Whatever you ask for in prayer, believe that you have received it, and it will be yours." However, "But when you ask, you must believe and not doubt, because the one who doubts is like a wave of the sea, blown and tossed by the wind. That person should not expect to receive anything from the Lord" (James 1:67 NIV). Refuse to let doubt be planted in your mind. For that to happen, be rooted in the Word. For example, look at how Jesus overcame the devil's temptation (Matthew 4:1–11) compared to his scheme with Eve in the Garden of Eden. By using the questioning factor (Genesis 3:1-5), Satan planted a seed of doubt in Eve's mind: "Did God really say you cannot eat from this garden?" In contrast to his encounter with Jesus, the devil used the ego factor.

The devil said that since He was the Son of God, He should have superpowers and be able to jump from this height. But Jesus recognized his tactic and responded, "It is also written: 'Do not put the Lord your God to the test'" (Matthew 4:7 NIV). Satan is cunning. He will keep trying to overpower the thoughts in your mind, but don't give in to his schemes. Rather hold on to your faith. "Truly I tell you, if you have faith as small as a mustard seed, you can say to this mountain, 'Move from here to there,' and it will move. Nothing will be impossible for you" (Matthew 17:20 NIV).

**Stagnant Mind:** This mindset is stuck in the past and cannot make progress in life. You find your mind moving in circles. Your thoughts circle back and forth on the memories of your past failures so that you can't think clearly to move past them, causing you to be discouraged and frustrated. To move forward out of this thought process, you need to form new thought patterns that will lead you in your desired direction, a new beginning, and a place of restoration. To break free from a stagnant mindset, continuously remind yourself that you are a new person. "This means that anyone who belongs to Christ has become a new person. The old life is gone; a new life has begun!" (2 Corinthians 5:17 NLT). New you, new Mindset! Be alert, God is about to do something new in your life. "Do not cling to events of the past or dwell on what happened long ago. Watch for the new thing I am going to do. It is happening already—you can see it now! I will make a road through the wilderness and give you streams of water there (Isaiah 43:18-19 GNT).

**Decide to transform your mind:** Now that you understand the value and power of the mind, it is easy to say that all you need to do is just think positively and everything will be fine. But how do you do that? You recognize that your mind is a battlefield, but do you know how to position yourself for divine opportunities? Taking hold of your mind's power holds the keys to your breakthrough.

Positive outcomes happen when you intentionally change the mental images in your mind to harbor what you desire. Note, even if you change your address, spouse, location, wardrobe, friends, and jobs but keep the same hurtful mindset, nothing will change in your life. A new outfit does not make a new person. However, a new mind brings a new perspective on living life. If things have not been as you expected, it is time to leave the old mindset behind and press forward with a new mindset. Do you happen to be discouraged, frustrated, hopeless, hurt, or unforgiveness? If yes, you need to acquire new thoughts toward restoration and a new beginning. You cannot get over past hurts until you first give up what you had in your mind.

In one of Abram's (whose name became Abraham) turning points, God told Abram He would give him the land as far as he could see (Genesis 13:14–15). Can you see far beyond your current circumstance? Search your mind. What challenges are you facing? Take inventory of your mind. *What type of mindset do you have? What do you need to remove to get closer to your goals?*

Do you believe what God has said concerning your situation? If yes, then things will begin to change in your favor. Do you know that God can make things happen out of season? Depend on God, starting with your thoughts. I pray this book will spur you to think and imagine new visions and ideas for your life, bigger and larger than ever imagined. Allow this seed to take root in your life, and watch God transform it into a wellspring of fruitful events. You are closer to achieving your goals than it looks. Get in agreement with God. "Don't copy the behavior and customs of this world, but let God transform you into a new person by changing the way you think. Then you will learn to know God's will for you, which is good and pleasing and perfect" (Romans 12:2 NLT).

**Ten Steps to Cultivating a Fertile Mind**

The mind is both a battlefield and a factory. Battles are won or defeated in the mind. The mind could also become a factory where products and ideas are born. Therefore, the crafty and cunning enemy tries to attack you first there. The enemy knows what purpose your goal will serve if it is achieved. And his goal is to steal, kill or destroy you and he will do whatever it takes to achieve this. So, to stop him you must counteract him with thoughts that line up with God's Word. Satan wants to attack the factory that will bring you joy, peace, and fulfillment with your family, career, health, children, education, or relationships.

Therefore, you must be healed in your mind before it can manifest physically. If you can win the battles in your mind, you have already won half the battle. Half is actualization, while the other fifty percent is the physical work that comes after. Serve the Lord with your mind, abiding by the steps below.

**1. Guard your heart.** Protect your mind from viruses and any contaminants. Computers need antivirus software to prevent trojans or any other malicious software attacks. This antivirus software also detects and can remove malware. *What are you using to scan, identify, protect, prevent, and delete your mind criminals?* Proverbs 4:23 (NIV) says, "Above all else, guard your heart, for everything you do flows from it." Everything you do encompasses all things, meaning it all passes through your mind. You must do everything possible to safeguard your mind.

Jesus used the weapon of the sword of the Spirit, God's Word, to defeat Satan's attacks in the wilderness after fasting for forty days. He quoted passages from the Old Testament. "It is written, man shall not live by bread alone, but by every word that proceeds out of the mouth of God" (Matthew 4:4 NKJV). "It is written; you shall not tempt the Lord your God" (Matthew 4:7 NKJV). "It is written; worship your Lord God and serve Him only" (Matthew 4:10 CSB). Against the three attacks of Satan, He used the sword of the Spirit, the Word of God, three times. When negative thoughts want to take over your mind, recite the Word of God that pertains to those thoughts. Find the Scripture that speaks to that situation and your goal, then use it consistently.

Guarding requires preparation before the battle arrives. It might require you to undergo rigorous physical training to discipline your body. It will also take a mind shift to want to go into the battle and be victorious. Know the battle that is ahead of you. Which giants do you need to face before you can achieve your goals? Do you have your spiritual weapons in place to defend yourself? As described in Ephesians 6:13-17, be alert and carry the full armor of God for protection in spiritual, mental, or physical battles.

*"Therefore, put on the full armor of God, so that when the day of evil comes, you may be able to stand your ground, and after you have done everything, to stand. Stand firm then, with the belt of truth buckled around your waist, the breastplate of righteousness in place, and your feet fitted with the readiness that comes from the gospel of peace. In addition, take up the shield of faith to extinguish all the flaming arrows of the evil one. Take the helmet of salvation and the sword of the Spirit, which is the word of God."*
–(Ephesians 6:13-17 NIV)

**2. Develop a courageous mindset.** To be victorious, you must have the courage to think beyond the parameters of your present space and moment. Do you have the courage to think beyond your present situation? Do you have the capacity to think positively about your current challenges? Like He was with Joshua in Joshua 1:3, God can give you every place you set your foot. *Do you know you are only one thought away from your breakthrough?* But you must be bold and courageous. "Be strong and of good courage, for to this people, you shall divide as an inheritance the land which I swore to their fathers to give them. Only be strong and very courageous, that you may observe to do according to all the law which Moses My servant commanded you; do not turn from it to the right hand or the left, that you may prosper wherever you go (Joshua 1:6-7 NKJV).

Trust God to make changes in your life. Decide in your mind to act courageously even if you do not feel it. Give Him something to anoint. A courageous mind is a faithful one. In the lesson of the three Hebrew men, Shadrach, Meshach, and Abednego, experience teaches us about standing firm even amid adversity, regardless of the status of the people involved (Daniel 3:16-18). Amid the burning fiery furnace, the three men acted courageously and focused on God regardless of the outcome. These men knew their God, trusted in His power to save them, refused to waiver in their faith, and made up their minds to be courageous.

**3. Change your perception.** Your perception determines your progression. If a problem does not change, you should change how you view it. *How have you perceived your goals and dreams?* In Numbers 13 and 14, do you notice the difference between the spies sent out by Moses to check out the land? Most of the spies were afraid of what they saw. They were defeated in their minds by the size of the people. Before the battle started, the spies had already lost just by sight. They had given up on going into battle. They could not see themselves challenging or overtaking the occupants of that land. However, one of the spies, Caleb, was not afraid. His perception and mindset were different from the others'. Caleb saw an exceedingly good land filled with opportunities to conquer. *What lens are you using to view your goals? What do you perceive as physical limitations? Can you perceive opportunities chasing you down?* Change your perception and let opportunities loom. The Lord is with you, no matter how huge your issue might seem. You are on the edge of your breakthrough. Don't be intimidated by what you see but be encouraged by what God says. Entertain new and positive perceptions that align with your goals.

As described in Carol Dweck's book titled Mindset: Changing the Way You think To Fulfill Your Potential, you can cultivate a growth mindset. She explains how the fixed and growth mindsets perceive the characteristics of skills, intelligence, efforts, feedback, concerns, criticism, results, challenges, and mistakes.

One mindset looks at a fixed potential at birth, while the other considers a developing growth potential. The growth mindset is what will position you to reach your goal.

**4. Continuously renew your mind.** Take account of the shutters in your mind. You hold the key to your mind. Who or what are you letting in your mind? If you don't control your mind, someone else will. Get rid of distractions, negative self-talk, and hurtful words others say. Throw away negative thoughts harboring anger, selfishness, hatred, fear, doubt, greed, jealousy, skepticism, vengeance, sadness, lust, and stress. Like a computer, delete unnecessary and harmful information to keep it safe and free from attacks. Clean out your mind's content and download and run the Jesus software. Fill your mind with Scripture: "Whatsoever things are true, whatsoever things are honest, whatsoever things are just, whatsoever things are pure, whatsoever things are lovely, whatsoever things are of good report; if there be any virtue, and if there be any praise, think on these things" (Philippians 4:8 KJV).

Renew your mind daily to be full of positive thoughts, such as joy, purity, peace, generosity, faith, abundance, kindness, gratitude, gentleness, love, patience, harmony, courage, and contentment. Change the concept of your mind by reconstructing it with positive information. First, find positive data that reveal facts about your goals and fill your mind with those thoughts.

*Are you stuck on the wrong images? Can you see yourself living in good health, full of energy, getting out of debt, or passing your exams?* Second Corinthians 10:5 (NKJV) says, "casting down arguments and every high thing that exalts itself against the knowledge of God, bringing every thought into captivity to the obedience of Christ."

To have authority over your mind, you need to protect your mind with the right imagination by surrounding yourself with images you want in your life. Regulate what you see and watch what enters your mind. Control what pictures you play in your mind. When negative thoughts want access to your mind, refute them and tune in to positive ones. It will take a couple of times of practice to master this but don't give up. Changing the channels of your mind by renewing it with life-affirming thoughts gives you authority. God says you will lend and not borrow, so imagine yourself in abundance, blessing others. Don't second-guess God's promises concerning you. Remember, don't give the enemy permission to torment your mind. We serve God with our minds too.

**5. Fill your mind with the Word of God.** Saturate your mind with the Word of God. Use His words as weapons of destruction to destroy every stronghold in your mind. For example, if you struggle with leadership, profess you are the head and not the tail from Deuteronomy 28:13.

Memorized Scriptures give me power and strength in the valley of despair. Here are my favorites:

- Psalm 119:11 NIV: "I have hidden your word in my heart that I might not sin against you."
- Philippians 4:13 NIV: "I can do all things through him who gives me strength."
- Romans 8:31 NIV: "If God is for us, who can be against us?"
- Romans 8:37 NIV: "No, in all these things we are more than conquerors through him who loved us. "
- 1 John 4:4: "The one who is in you is greater than the one who is in the world."
- Joshua 1:8-9 NKJV: "This Book of the Law shall not depart from your mouth, but you shall meditate in it day and night, that you may observe to do according to all that is written in it.

> For then you will make your way prosperous, and then you will have good success. Have I not commanded you? Be strong and of good courage; do not be afraid, nor be dismayed, for the Lord your God is with you wherever you go."

God promises that those who meditate on the Word of God and fill their minds with it will be prosperous and successful. Therefore, I meditate and profess God's Word when negative thoughts haunt me. In a crisis, it is beneficial if you have memorized the Word of God and stored it in your mind. You can cultivate a positive mindset and overcome negative thoughts by reciting the Scriptures.

**6. Practice gratitude and praise.** Attract what you want by thanking God for them before achieving those goals. "Pray continually, give thanks in all circumstances; for this is God's will for you in Christ Jesus" (1 Thessalonians 5:17-18 NIV). In every circumstance, such as loneliness, sadness, happiness, fear, weakness, infirmities, poverty, or riches, find something to be grateful for and praise Him for all the blessings you have experienced and His daily grace.

In Acts 16:25-34, Paul and Silas, preaching the gospel, were falsely accused, arrested, and imprisoned. Instead of getting depressed, they prayed and sang songs of praise to God even in their darkest hour. Then a miracle took place. Suddenly, a violent earthquake shook the foundation of the prison, and the doors opened, chains were broken, and the two men walked out free.

Even if you can't change what happened in the past, i.e., the divorce, heartbreak, failed exam, medical report, or job loss, please note that you can choose how you respond to your current and future conditions by rejoicing in all situations.

Prophet Habakkuk rejoiced at his lowest point when his land was not fruitful (Habakkuk 3:17-18). I heard the story of a pastor who was diagnosed as infertile, and he found himself praying for others wanting children, and those people would give birth to their babies. He was bombarded with baby ceremonies and photos on social media during this time, desiring this very blessing. It wasn't until he got to a point where he started rejoicing with those who already had what they desired that he received his breakthrough. Though it took him six years to get to that point, he finally achieved his goal of becoming a father. Now he and his wife are blessed with three children. Cultivate the habit of always rejoicing.

7.   **Choose your associations.** Who or what you surround yourself with indicates who you are and in what direction you might be heading. Can your current connections keep you accountable for your goals? Can they cheer you on when you share your goals and dreams? Do not be deceived. "Bad company corrupts good character" (1 Corinthians 15:33 NLT). Watch the company you keep and abstain from all things incongruent with your goals. Be extremely careful of the books you read, the movies you watch, the social media platforms you indulge in, or the conversations you have in your mind or with others. Surround yourself with positive influences and watch how your mind transforms. "Don't copy the behavior and customs of this world, but let God transform you into a new person by changing the way you think" (Romans 12:2 NLT).

8.   **Profess your desires.** Feed your goals by speaking life to them. Align your mind with what you profess. Don't profess one thing and think differently. Be disciplined in your thought life. Be specific and clear on what you want. Find a scripture that speaks to what you want to happen in your life and repeat it daily. Engrave it

on your heart, phone, car, room, or office, and then wait patiently for the Lord to honor His Word. For example:

- Are you feeling sad? Say, "This is the day the Lord has made, I'll rejoice and be glad in it" (Psalm 118:24 NKJV).
- Maybe you struggle with directions. Say, "In all my ways, I acknowledge and recognize you, Father. Make my paths straight" (Proverbs 3:6). "Father, thank You, 'for your plans for me are for good and not evil'" (Jeremiah 29:11).
- Do you have self-doubt? "I can do all things through Christ who strengthens me" (Philippians 4:13 NKJV).

**9. Be committed.** Commit yourself to what you want to create by using a godly mindset to build and develop your goals. Do not waiver from the new strategies you have learned. If perhaps you do, get right back to it and continue. Create new habits along the lines of what you want. Maybe you can start your day with an I-can-do attitude; embody and visualize having that peaceful and pleasant day. The way you think is the way you feel. Organize your body, emotions, energies, and ecosystem in the new direction, and stick to it.

**10. Do not quit!** Your mind is a powerful tool in the hand of God, the goal redeemer. Please don't waste it. You must have authority over your thoughts to live a fruitful life. A receiving mind is like fertile soil prepared for the planting season. In this season of your life, decide to remove distractions, think positively and creatively, and watch the magnificent outcomes. Apply your mind to change situations by intentionally and consciously directing your thoughts toward your desired outcome.

Ultimately, remember that you are one thought away from your victory. Do you have the capacity to think? To achieve what you've never done, think of what you've never thought about. Acquire new thoughts! Build the courage to look beyond your current drawbacks and watch the transformation that follows. I pray that you'll be awakened to a whole new life of power and divine opportunities as you do so. God will break down those mighty walls that have been delaying you from getting your breakthrough and reaching your full potential. Now is your time. Reading this book at this time of your life is not coincidental.

---

**Moving Forward**

**Self-awareness:** Practice self-inquiry. Learn to decipher your feelings, emotions, thought processes, and mind's content. Take note of the patterns of desirable and undesirable occurrences in your life. What mindset is attributed to those results? How can you build new patterns to start thinking differently?

**Affirming words:** Examine the season you are in right now. Establish your goals. Search for words that speak life to those goals and that area of your life. Use those words to direct the outcome you want and debunk any myths. Memorize and speak those words out loud as frequently as possible.

**Feed your thoughts:** Check the contents of your mind to see if it is consistent with life-affirming words, such as "I am the head and not the tail" (Deuteronomy 28:13). "He that is in me is greater than he who is in the world" (1 John 4:4). I am an overcomer.

Continuously feed your thoughts with your goal-affirming words. Let them dominate your life. Practice self-talk. The more you feed your mind with positive thoughts, the better you are re-energized to face your tasks. You will have the can-do attitude needed to crush every obstacle.

**Change your perception:** Look at your past and current mistakes as learning opportunities. Recognize the silver lining and look at those situations positively differently. Please do not loathe defeat. Instead, envision where you want to be and believe you can reach it. Remember to first create what you want in your mind to make room for manifestation.

PART III

# Act Intentionally Toward Achieving Your Goals

*"Everything you think, say, and do needs to become intentional and aligned with your purpose, your values, and your goals."*
—Jack Canfield

CHAPTER 9

# Principle 7
# Manage Your Time and Avoid Procrastination

*"There is a time for everything, and a season for every activity under the heavens."*
(Ecclesiastes 3:1 NIV)

Time is the currency of life. No matter what anyone can do, there are only twenty-four hours a day, and no one can add more time to their day or subtract from it. How well you spend your time determines your progression in life. Are you in charge of those twenty-four hours? Even if you are not in charge, time goes by while you still decide what to do.

The core of my successes is predicated on proficient time management. I value my time and other people's time. I won't waste your time, and I won't let people waste mine. If I have an appointment and run three minutes late, I alert the person involved. That's the same expectation I have from others. Because I could use the lateness to work on something valuable, time can only be spent once, and any time lost cannot be purchased back. Are you getting value out of your time? If not, stop wasting time and act now. Before a goal is achieved, time must be invested in making plans, setting goals, and executing actionable tasks to bring about its success. Time management is a necessary discipline for success in life. People with good time management skills experience happiness, success, efficiency, productivity, reduced stress levels, and educational achievement.

> *"Time is the coin of your life.*
> *It is the only coin you have,*
> *and only you can determine how it will be spent.*
> *Be careful lest you let other people spend it for you."*
> —Carl Sandburg

God is a God of time and seasons. It took the Israelites forty years to get to the Promised Land, a journey that could have taken just eleven days. During those years, God demonstrated His power and executed His strategic plan to get them to the land flowing with milk and honey. He made deliberate decisions and appropriately selected the right people, like Moses and Joshua. Likewise, God designed the appointed time to bring Jesus to earth. Nothing God did was a coincidence. God is a master time manager!

Anyone who suffers from poor time management is at risk of not developing their inherent potential. Such people face the risk of stunting their growth in life. They are like a river flowing wherever the current directs it, without a destination. Having no sense of direction leads to nowhere in life. These people barely experience acceleration in their careers or relationships. Moving forward seems foreign to them because they are accustomed to moving in circles, running backward, or just remaining stagnant.

Warning signs of poor time management include memory problems, an inability to concentrate, poor judgment, anxious or racing thoughts, constant worrying, moodiness, irritability, agitation, an inability to relax, feeling overwhelmed, and unhappiness. Managing your time is essential to reaching your full potential. Fortunately, the skill of managing time can be learned.

According to the U.S. Bureau of Labor Statistics 2020 data, the average time used by women ages fifteen to seventy-five was 41.2 percent sleeping or grooming, 21.3 percent leisure, 12.3 percent household activities and care, 10.4 percent work activities, and 4.4 percent eating.

Spend some time accounting for the average time you spend in these areas. Your objective is to find how to maneuver time from one activity to an area that would create time to work on your goal. You can expect to double your productivity when you learn to manage your time efficiently and handle it with intentionality. Determine to do what it takes to manage your time effectively if you want to experience sustainable results.

Be open to new patterns. Some of your goals may require you to get up earlier than usual. In writing this book, I exercised discipline to wake up a few hours earlier than my regular time to write every day except for weekends. I strategically dedicated mornings to writing while my kids were still in bed, and there was less distraction, i.e., no incoming emails or phones ringing. Implement an effective pattern for executing tasks and a code of conduct in your daily activities, and your increased productivity will be inevitable. One of my codes of conduct is to honor people's time by efficiently communicating any lateness. Another one of my codes of conduct is to reward myself after completing tasks on my goal list. I won't indulge in extracurricular activities such as answering phone calls, watching TV, or engaging in conversations with in-house family members until after executing my tasks.

Assess how you use your time.

**Time Assessment**

1. How do you spend your time daily, i.e., sleeping, caring for others, working, leisure, eating, household activities, travel, social media, emails and phone calls?
2. Examine your schedule. What are you in the habit of doing daily?
3. What is your routine? Identify your areas of inconsistency.
4. What are your time-wasters? List all the things you usually do on weekdays and weekends.
5. What are the patterns you want to break?
6. Look into your future. What new habits or patterns do you want to implement?
7. Who or what are the beneficiaries of your managed time? List them. These people or things will motivate you to stay on track.
8. How do you envision things being different in the future?
9. What can you do right now to move in the direction of achieving a tangible goal? Then do it.

Understanding your habits and past actions can help you be aware of when those habits start to enter your life again. This simple awareness will help you crush them.

> "You will never 'find' time for anything. If you want time, you must make it."
> –Charles Bruxton

My philosophy about time is that I won't let time control me, but rather, I will control it. Learn to master your time. Remember, the better you manage your time, the more you will experience predictable outcomes. Are you one to overextend yourself or one who cannot say "no" to people? Do you always have a full schedule and find yourself running from one place to another? The way to manage such a dilemma is never to over-commit yourself—schedule meetings with ample time to take mental breaks. Effective time management entails having balance. Maintaining a work-life balance is a continuous process. Decide daily to win by having a productive time in which you achieve your tasks.

Once you set a target goal, construct your schedule with some downtime. I schedule almost every one of my tasks, including my sleep time, shopping, cooking, and hangout duration. When I hit my target for a particular task, my downtime could be spent listening to music or making phone calls. Depending on the task, I like my downtime to move toward the goal, meaning that my phone calls could be to chat with a friend about the task to gain more insights or to solicit feedback. However, commit to a daily routine that allows you to achieve everything on your schedule but leaves wiggle room for unknown circumstances.

Do not be afraid if your set schedule changes and you lose time; quickly re-strategize your plans. While accomplishing career goals like grant writing, I have encountered times when I would have to seek assistance picking up my children from school to finish a task. But there are times when that's not the case. My hairstylist shares a similar philosophy with me on time management, but her co-worker, Tisha, is still working on managing her clients when they do not keep their appointments. Early one Saturday morning in the summer, Tisha's client scheduled a three-hour hairdo but was a no-show.

Aside from charging a no-show fee, which, in this case, she found out the client's card on file declined, it's good practice to learn to pivot and revise your schedule swiftly should you encounter roadblocks like this. If possible, account for the loss of time and move to the next item on your schedule or maintain a backup list that I call "filler tasks." These are tasks that are not time-sensitive, such as any would-like-to-do items. I have tasks like "look for a lost flash drive" on my running list of filler tasks. On that list, I have hospitality emails or phone calls that I like to make. Maintain your list; it will come in handy whenever you have an opening in your schedule. You can use an app like Apple or Samsung Notes, Google Calendar, or Todoist to maintain your task list.

Below are specific strategies for good time management.

**Strategies for Managing Your Time**

1. **Set clear and realistic goals.** What would you like to achieve? Write down one goal at a time. Be specific. State what you want with no ambiguity. Separate your long-term goals from your short-term goals. Devise daily, weekly, and monthly tasks that would support your short-term goals. Carry your written goals with you every day. Before going to bed, pull out your next day's schedule and imagine how the tasks will be executed. This practice reveals any kinks in your plans, and your mind will work hard to provide potential solutions. When you wake up, go over your day's schedule again before getting out of bed or leaving the house.

**SMART Goal Reality Check**

    a. Can you specifically and clearly define your goal?
    b. Is your goal measurable?

c. Will your goal have observable evidence with quantifiable outcomes? If not, add a quantifiable scale. For example, in six months, I would have lost eighteen pounds.
d. Think through your goal and ask yourself if it is attainable, knowing your background and based on experience. Who would you hire, or what resources would you need to complete a task?
e. Are the needed people and resources within your reach or control?
f. Can you break your goals into small, actionable tasks?
g. Next, ask yourself if your goal is relevant to your mission. If not, make it so.
h. Finally, set a realistic time limit or deadline to achieve this goal.

If you answer "no" to questions e and f, you might need to set an initial goal that must be achieved before proceeding with your original goal. You have written a SMART goal if your goal captures all these questions. Frequently monitor your progress and freely adjust your timeline and expectations. The rule is to continue reviewing, reevaluating, and revising your goals for misalignment until you have reached them.

2. **Prioritize your tasks.** One of the successful strategies used to prioritize tasks is the four-quadrant "Eisenhower Decision Matrix," derived from the task management principles of the former president Dwight D. Eisenhower. The method was further developed by Stephen Covey, Roger, and Rebecca Merrill. Covey explains, "Most of us spend too much time on what is urgent and not enough time on what is important." Imagine how productive you will be if you are able to balance your urgent tasks with the important

ones. Sometimes important tasks can become urgent if care is not taken.

My husband gets on me about driving my car empty of gas before refilling it. He fills his car's tank whenever the gauge indicates a quarter full to avoid an urgent situation. Occasionally, I will forget that my tank is on "E" and has the zero-mile indicator flashing for my attention. I wish my car had a voice-powered co-pilot technology system to audibly alert me whenever the car fuel is low until I refuel it, similar to the annoying but effective seatbelt warning. During those situations, I pray to God for a miracle to quickly get to the nearest gas station without my car stopping. And, of course, it just so happens that the gas station is always miles away. In those moments, God reminds me to practice the "quarter tank rule" to balance my important tasks effectively and prevent them from becoming urgent. Urgent tasks are time sensitive, such as paying a bill or attending meetings. In contrast, important tasks are responsibilities that are valuable to reaching your goals, like working out or taking a cooking class, for instance.

To manage your time effectively and efficiently, you want to evaluate your tasks and categorize them using the Eisenhower Decision Matrix. This four-quadrant matrix categorizes your tasks as Urgent/Not Urgent and Important/Not Important, followed by allocating your respective tasks in each quadrant in their order of importance versus urgency.

- In Quadrant 1 (Q1), list Important and Urgent tasks. Focus on these tasks and do them first.
- In Quadrant 2 (Q2), list Important and Not Urgent tasks. Limit and schedule these tasks.
- In Quadrant 3 (Q3), list Not Important and Urgent tasks. Manage and delegate these tasks.

- In Quadrant 4 (Q4), list Not Important and Not Urgent tasks. Avoid or eliminate these tasks.

|  | Urgent | Not Urgent |
|---|---|---|
| **Important** | **Q1.** Do tasks first | **Q2.** Schedule tasks for later |
| **Not Important** | **Q3.** Delegate tasks to others | **Q4.** Avoid tasks |

Quadrants 1 and 2 are the two "Important" tasks located at the top, with Quadrant 1 listing the "Urgent" items while Quadrant 2 lists the "Not Urgent" ones. The "Not Important" tasks are located at the bottom quadrants as Quadrants 3 and 4, with Quadrant 3 listing the "Urgent" tasks and Quadrant 4 containing the "Not Urgent" items.

After allocating your tasks in each quadrant, you want to execute items in Quadrant I, your Important and Urgent activities, i.e., medical appointments and picking up children from school. Minimize plans in Quadrant 2, the Not Urgent but Important items like vacation planning and exercising. Schedule these tasks and be careful not to procrastinate. However, be sure to manage and delegate activities in Quadrant 3, your "Urgent" but "Not Important" items. These are interruptions or other people's urgent tasks. Outsource services or use tools like Microsoft Power Automate to complete business tasks. You want to avoid or eliminate the "Not Important" and "Not Urgent" matters in Quadrant 4, such as unessential activities like watching TV, superfluous shopping, and social media. These are mere distractions and time wasters.

3. **Take action.** No matter how many plans you make, if you do not take action by doing, you will not move toward reaching your goal. Some people have big dreams and no actions to back them up. Once your plans and activities have been prioritized, please act. You want to group similar tasks and break down larger tasks into smaller executable ones. Then, on a daily basis, make a to-do list in order of priority and set time limits. Execute the most urgent and important ones first. This way, you train yourself to be proactive rather than reactive.

> *"The great dividing line between success and failure can be expressed in five words: 'I did not have time.'"*
> –Franklin Field

The hardest part of taking action is getting started, so begin with small, bite-sized milestones. Once you accomplish the smaller tasks, you will get motivated to complete the entire task. The key is to be disciplined with your time. You also want to know the time of day your energy is most expended. Advocate for your time by letting people around you know what you are doing to stay on track. When I am in my writing phase, I notify my regular contacts so that they can expect minimal interactions during these periods. Automatic response emails and text messages work well for notifications. Most people will respect your time once you communicate your schedule.

And they may help you reduce distractions while you complete those tasks. Meanwhile, you might need to put your phone on silent mode or refrain from going to places where you are likely to run into people you know.

If you need an accountability partner, get one. This person should be a conscientious individual (described in Chapter 11) capable of holding you responsible and monitoring your progress. It might be a mentor, a coach, a co-worker, a family member, or a friend. Share your goals and schedule with them. Discuss the frequency of contact and the approach that will work best for you. Let them know your SMART goal, your whys, and what you desire from them while you work on accomplishing your goal and the changes you plan to make. For example, if you will be taking a night class, you can say, "Please remember that I won't be accessible on these days during these hours." And you may propose an accountable request, like sharing a lesson learned and an actionable item from the class.

Overall, stay proactive and not reactive. Ensure your actions align with your priorities, and learn to say "no" to other people's priorities.

4. **Develop a routine.** To achieve your goal, you should create a sustainable routine that will make you work toward completing goals on time. If you want new results, you must change your old approach. Develop a daily ritual from morning to evening that prepares your mind and body for a new habit. It takes about sixty-six days to form a new habit, so be prepared to stick to this routine for weeks before you can expect mastery. This routine could involve memorizing Scriptures, meditations, exercises, journaling, or affirmations you partake in as soon as you wake up.

Changing your patterns includes modifying the foods you consume, activities like driving routes, parking spaces, or your process of winding down at the end of your day. Whatever you do, develop a routine that keeps your time accountable.

5. **Delegate or outsource tasks**. To stay on task in a timely fashion, assess to whom you can reliably delegate or offload some of your tasks. Is there anyone in your unit or chain of command you can trust to execute the task? If you do not have any, consider hiring some help. When I began to prioritize my weekend tasks, I figured if I could get help with getting my house cleaned and clothes washed, it would free up a significant portion of time to get other important tasks done, so I hired a housekeeper to manage my house chores.

> *"Either you run the day, or the day runs you."*
> –Jim Rohn

6. **Use a calendar.** In order to be accountable and organized, use a reputable calendar to create your tasks, lists, schedules, events, and reminders. Every Android and iOS device comes equipped with a calendar app, and there are calendar planner journals with time and date entries. Pick your preference and stick to it. I use my journals to write my yearly goals, then I use my phone for my daily tasks.

You can easily set your calendar on electronic devices to notify yourself of upcoming tasks with different reminder time intervals. My notifications are typically set a week in advance, followed by a day, then thirty- or fifteen-minute reminders depending on the type of event. The Google mobile calendar app even allows you to separate events from tasks. I like the task feature because once you complete it, you can mark it as done and it will automatically be crossed out. Seeing a task checked off or crossed out produces an incredible feeling of accomplishment. Please do not forget to block out personal time and allow flexibility in your schedule. In some cases of attention deficit disorder (ADD) or attention deficit hyperactivity disorder (ADHD), professional diagnosis and treatment of the disorder may be necessary to help with focus.

> *"Never leave that 'till tomorrow, which you can do today."*
> –Benjamin Franklin

7. **Avoid procrastination.** Examine why you prefer to delay or put off a task until it's due or past due. For some, it could be self-limiting beliefs, a feeling of inadequacy, lack of motivation, self-control or discipline, or being overwhelmed with too many tasks or overcommitted. If procrastination is not dealt with, it can lead to wasted time, unproductivity, stress, panic attacks, anxiety, or worry.

**Steps to Help You Stop Procrastinating**

1. **Recognize why you procrastinate.** The ability to get to the source of why you procrastinate is one of the primary factors in taking control and stopping the habit. An example of a source of procrastination is being a perfectionist and always being unsatisfied with an outcome if the task is not executed exactly how you want it.

It could also be that you typically agonize over things that are not within your control. For others, it could be a lack of interest in the task. If that's the case, get something that will motivate you. If your case is that you have too many tasks, then focus on how you need to reduce them by either not accepting to do some tasks or delegating them to others. If you procrastinate because you lack resources, guidance, knowledge, or direction, then seek to gain these things as soon as possible before embarking on or committing to those goals.

> *"By prevailing over all obstacles and distractions,
> one may unfailingly arrive at his chosen goal or destination."*
> –Christopher Columbus

2. **Identify your time wasters and reduce them**. Paraphrasing Christopher Columbus's quote on reaching your goal, you have a chance to arrive at your stated goals if you can prevail over your hindrances and distractions. Sometimes we delay acting on our goals by using other menial tasks to avoid the real ones. Identify your time wasters. These are distracting actions you indulge in to avoid executing your primary goals. My biggest distraction is my phone notifications, so I simply turn them off when I am serious about completing a task.

To act timely and prevail over procrastination, eliminate distractions when possible. Some people's distraction or time waster is diverting attention to a good cause instead of working on their goals. When you have a pending task, you would rather spend time cleaning your house, which is an important but not urgent task, to avoid or delay a higher priority task. Are you always looking for the right time, which never seems to come before you start working on a task? Limiting your time frames might help you overcome this hurdle of never finding the right time to work on a task. Once you recognize your time wasters, devise a strategy that keeps you from indulging in less important tasks.

3. **Implement a working strategy.** Several strategies to avoid procrastination have been published. One of Brian Tracy's books suggests identifying and eating your frog first, which means tackling your most challenging and important task early to give you the

motivation and energy to proceed to the less demanding tasks. This practice is consistent with Mark Twain's statement below.

> *"Eat a live frog every morning
> and nothing worse will happen
> to you the rest of the day."*
> –Mark Twain

Another strategy mentioned earlier is to break your large tasks into small bite-sizes that are manageable. This strategy works when a task seems impossible. But if you break it into manageable sizes, you can conquer one of the tasks at a time until you finish what seemed overwhelming. One strategy is using the reward system to motivate you to embark on and finish a task, i.e., taking breaks or going for a spa treatment.

You decide to get a treat after making a significant contribution or completing what you are supposed to do. You could be unmotivated to execute a task and would rather watch an episode of your favorite show. Your devised strategy should be to negotiate with yourself to watch your show after you have completed the task. Another strategy is to unsubscribe from your distractions. For instance, you might need to turn off your cell phones and television, deactivate social media accounts, or limit interaction with others to complete a task.

In graduate school, some of my peers deactivated their Facebook accounts during their dissertation writing phase because it distracted them from fully committing to their writing process. That was their way of disciplining themselves. What are your distractions? Identify yours and work on reducing or eliminating them. Start by reducing your distractions first and see how well you perform. Then examine whether your distractor is serving you at all. If the answer is "no," eliminate it.

4. **Practice self-discipline.** Follow your to-do list as written in your calendar. If it's time to send that email, do it as soon as your notification comes up to avoid interruptions. Control the urge not to deviate from your action plans. Put your customized strategies for avoiding time wasters and procrastination to work. Practice the discipline that allows you to stay on track. Develop a mindset of absolute determination and believe you can do what you set out to do. Do it diligently. Visualize the outcome of your tasks and then take action. Discipline yourself to commit to spending fifteen minutes per day on the task. If you fail, forget, or fall short, forgive yourself, start again, and recommit yourself. The most important thing is to do something and not do nothing.

5. **Recruit help.** Seek support from people who have the skills to keep you accountable and support you through your process of learning how to use your time effectively. Inform them of your goals, priorities, and timeline, and let them help you.

> *"The key is not to prioritize what's on your schedule but to schedule your priorities."*
> –Stephen Covey

In sum, time management is a learned skill that requires conscious and consistent efforts to develop. You may encounter multiple failed attempts. If you do not give up, you are bound to triumph over them. Execute your actionable plans, which will carry you to the finish line. Remember that God has never lost a battle. Walk with Him as He walks with you through your process of overcoming procrastination.

## Moving Forward

**Annual activity:** Make a list of your goals, prioritizing them from the most important to the least. Starting with the most important, write out your SMART goal. Compile images that represent all your goals for the year. Create a vision board that displays the outcome you want for that year. These could be photos found in newspapers, magazines, or online. You can also use an applicable quote written or typed on paper. Get a package of large card stock paper, scissors, and glue. Cut out the photos and glue them on the cardstock paper. Feel free to accessorize the paper as you want. Once this activity is completed, place it strategically in a room or location you will see daily. Better yet, take a photo of your completed vision board using your phone and use it as your screensaver. This way, you can carry the mental images of your goals with you. The visualization of your goals is a proven method of achieving them. Alternatively, you can create a digital vision board from scratch by pasting online images on a Microsoft PowerPoint presentation, Word document, or any other preferred design template.

**Monthly activity:** Obtain a goal worksheet and clearly define your intentions for that month. Start by identifying your specific tasks, how to measure your progress, the resources you will need, your potential obstacles, and proposed solutions. Write down the steps you need to take to overcome your obstacles. Now, break down your specific and attainable monthly goal into weekly tasks. Get a calendar and add those tasks in the order of priority. Set the reminders on your calendar to the frequency of your choice. Don't forget to enter your events as well.

**Daily activity**: Stop the habits of unstructured routines with your time. Know exactly what you are supposed to do, when, and where you are doing it. A to-do list will help you structure your daily activities and accomplish your tasks. The night before, write out all the activities for the next day on your calendar. Set the notifications to remind you at least thirty minutes before the start time and, if necessary, an additional ten minutes before the event begins. Use your calendar for starting a task if it has an embedded countdown feature. Please remember to set aside some time for yourself to take a break. As you complete a task, cross it out or remove it from your list. Should you not accomplish a task for one reason or another, move the unfinished task forward.

**Stay focused:** Recognize your interference. These are things that interfere with accomplishing your tasks during the day. Resist distractions and procrastination by any means necessary. These interferences and distractions could come from your emotional state, phone calls, watching TV, and interruptions from family, colleagues, or even strangers. Find strategies to help you develop discipline with your time, try them out, and implement the ones that work for you. If you make your strategy a routine, your self-control capacity will expand.

**CHAPTER 10**

# Principle 8
# Be Self-Motivated

*"I can do all things through him who gives me strength."*
(Philippians 4:13 NIV)

Have you ever experienced a time when you not only had the energy to finish a chore but also mustered more energy to execute some unplanned ones? This determination to continue is the drive you need to accomplish all your tasks, even when they may seem unnecessary.

Now imagine being able to re-engineer that level of commitment all the time. How wonderful would life be if you were always on fire to successfully knock out all you set out to do? Self-motivation is your ability to drive actions and resilience to produce even amid challenges.

Our drive to perform is often inspired internally, externally, or a combination of the two. I know whenever my third-grader is helping around the house without being prompted, I can expect a compensation discussion afterward. Could my son's action be considered self-motivation?

Extrinsic or intrinsic motivation influences our driving force and desire to perform. Extrinsic motivation is governed by factors outside of you. For instance, a career or job motivates many to perform because they expect a paycheck after working. You get motivated to wake up early to prepare for the job. The motivation to keep going is interrupted if the job is taken away. Situations like this remind me of people who, because they got fired, lost their drive to get out of bed, eat, or clean up after themselves. These people's detachment from their jobs sets them back and debilitates them.

On the other hand, intrinsic motivation is innately driven by your desires, contentment, and personal growth. Intrinsic motivation is where self-motivation takes place—that desire to achieve a goal despite the opposition; you know you can rise above it. Being self-motivated gives you a relentless determination to pursue and accomplish your goals. It fuels your energy to succeed. When we operate from a place of passion, values, and belief systems, we are motivated to keep going regardless of whether we get paid.

Now imagine if you could tie your goals to being intrinsically motivated. The outcome you will receive will be fulfilling. For example, although I teach for a living, I know that is my calling domain. I volunteer at different organizations where I teach for free. It is my ministry. I love what I do and serve the Lord through my calling. This concept aligns with Mark Twain's quote, "Find a job you enjoy doing, and you will never have to work a day in your life." Don't get me wrong; there are days when I get frustrated, tired, and weak about what I do, but I get back up again, fix my eyes on the author and finisher of my faith, and continue to labor in His vineyard. The book of Hebrews emphasizes that stumbling occurs when our focus shifts from Jesus to our circumstances or anything else. However, to live effectively, the key is "looking unto Jesus, the author and finisher of our faith, who for the joy that was set before Him endured the cross, despising the shame, and has sat down at the right hand of the throne of God" (Hebrews 12:2 NKJV).

As believers, the assurance that we have victory over every circumstance we encounter is a motivator to strive to live life to our full potential. This knowledge should give you the confidence to achieve whatever you desire because you trust your goal redeemer, Jesus, to help bear the burden so you can persevere through your life challenges. First John 5:4–5 (AMP) says, "For everyone born of God is victorious and overcomes the world; and this is the victory that has conquered and overcome the world—our continuing, persistent faith in Jesus the Son of God." You are a conqueror. Through Christ, you can defeat every challenge on your path.

Self-motivation might appear as a sporadic moment for some, while others have mastered maintaining momentum over time. Learning what motivates you and staying motivated are keys to successfully achieving goals.

First, know who you are. Examine the "Sixteen Basic Desires in the Reiss Profile" in the *"Who Am I?"* book by Steven Reiss. He describes how basic desires or motives inspire your end goals. Those desires are power, independence, curiosity, acceptance, order, saving, honor, idealism, social contact, family, status, vengeance, romance, eating, physical exercise, and tranquility. For example, if your goal is to be physically fit, your desire for that would be *physical exercise*. Likewise, the desire would be for order if you want to achieve cleanliness, stability, or organization.

In agreement with Ran Zilca, goals with built-in motivations are most likely to be attained since we already have an invested desire and an existing passion. God has given us the grace to accomplish what we are committed to. Every year, I fast for forty days and stay away from solid foods from six in the morning to six in the evening. My goal for the fast is to seek God's face for my spiritual well-being. My fasting periods are like retreats with God and me alone. I use lunch times to go for a walk and hold deep conversations. The first week is the most challenging period, because I am often expected to participate in work or social events involving food and treats. I can sacrifice not eating during these times because I am motivated to pray and meditate.

*"The goals you are most likely to accomplish are the ones that have motivation built into them, meaning you don't have to talk yourself into pursuing them because you naturally have the passion to do so."*
—Ran Zilca

Going through the sixteen desires will help you identify your desire pattern and better understand how to navigate your goals to completion. Determine which four or five combinations of desires are most meaningful to you. These desires are your core values. They will fuel you throughout the process of establishing your goals. One of my core values (Reiss's basic desire) is *independence*, which motivates me to want to seek freedom and be autonomous. That drives me to be knowledgeable enough so that I won't have to rely on others to get work done. The intrinsic desire to have freedom and be self-reliant guides my actions and accomplishments. Know your motives.

Motivation moves you to act. Action is needed to accomplish tasks. If your commitment level is high, you are less likely to disengage from a task. The commitment is there if the outcome is associated with a prize or if it produces fulfillment. To be motivated, the benefit of the goal must meet a need in your life. For instance, if your goal is to work and earn a certain income so that you and your family can maintain a buoyant lifestyle, then your motivation to work meets the need for housing, accommodation, and food allowance necessary for surviving. A focus on the outcome would motivate you to go through the process of achieving that goal.

Two professors of psychology, Edward Deci and Richard Ryan, defined achievement through intrinsic motivation as meeting three innate physiological needs: competence, autonomy, and connection or relatedness, which is the self-determination theory. When these basic needs are satisfied, they either produce increased self-motivation or lead to diminished motivation when those needs are unmet.

I perform better and experience optimum function when a complex task is attributed to Reiss motives. Since I am motivated by independence, I learned that earning a college degree could bring financial freedom and stability at a young age, so I pursued it. Even when I encountered obstacles with tuition, passing a class, or registering for courses, I stuck through them. I wanted my independence badly enough to remain focused on my end goal.

In college, I encountered two friends who valued having children more. They got out of college and started a family when the opportunity presented itself. Your belief systems should support your core value. Due to my spirituality, I value bringing people to the knowledge of God as the supreme being and helping them reach their full potential. Therefore, my driving force with my women's empowerment ministry and writing this book is to motivate others to achieve their goals through reliance on our goal redeemer, Jesus, and to use proven strategies to drive action.

Human motivation occurs in a particular order, as postulated by Abraham H. Maslow in 1943. His general-dynamic theory of human motivation was based on clinical experience and summarized in a pyramid form. Human motivations typically move from the lowest level, starting with physiological needs, safety and security, love and belongingness, and self-esteem, to self-actualization and self-transcendence at the pyramid's peak. To aim for the highest level, which is the state of self-actualization, one must realize their full potential and gain fulfillment. You must fulfill the lower needs first, like the physiological needs, before moving up to self-esteem and self-actualization. Intrinsic motivation is the result of a desire to satisfy these needs.

Self-efficacy is also very important for self-motivation. While motivation is the desire to achieve a goal, self-efficacy, as defined by psychologist Albert Bandura, is the set of beliefs driving your "ability to succeed in specific situations or accomplish a task." This capability can provide a source of self-motivation and cognitive strength for goal fulfillment. People with high levels of self-efficacy can recover from failures quickly, have the resilience to experience stress while still living healthy lifestyles, and have high chances of achieving their goals.

> *"People's beliefs about their abilities have a profound effect on those abilities."*
> –Albert Bandura

While levels of self-efficacy could be innate, they can also be developed in healthy individuals through one's interpretation of these five sources of influence:

1. Vicarious experiences via other people's performances could appear as role models.
2. Physiological feedback from bodily sensations consumes your emotional, physical, and physiological states.

3. Verbal persuasion is one's ability to perform through words of encouragement.
4. Performance outcomes are based on the success of previous mastery experiences.
5. Imaginal experiences, which is the art of visualizing yourself being successful. As proposed by James Maddux in 2013, the fifth source is imaginal experiences gained through visualization of your goals as being achievable. This source explains the concept of "vision boarding" to clarify our goals.

Maintaining a high level of motivation attracts a self-fulfilling prophecy, meaning a person's beliefs or expectations become true because their behavior reinforces the belief. Combining your expectations with your behavior yields a powerful force for acting on your goals and achieving them. Your proclamations through self-fulfilling prophecy will induce effort and performance for you to achieve a desirable outcome.

Please note that you must believe in yourself for the self-fulfilling prophecy to work. Also, consider that you are worthy of achieving your goals and know that no one besides you is responsible for your growth. God has already given you all you need to thrive in life. However, it would be best if you were your authentic self.

Get started by knowing yourself. *Who are you? What motivates you?* Recognize and be in harmony with your past experiences and old belief systems, then walk through your stumbling blocks one at a time. Get a journal, create a vision for the new person you are becoming, and establish realistic plans for acquiring what you want from life. If you can conceive the dream, believe in it, and nurture it, you can birth it. The same is true for every one of your goals.

Employ proven strategies that can develop your self-motivation. Positive thinking and proclamations are essential tools. There are promises from the Scriptures that you can start mastering. Build immunity to negative thoughts and self-defeating prophecies.

Proverbs 18:21 (AMP) says, "Death and life are in the power of the tongue, And those who love it and indulge it will eat its fruit and bear the consequences of their words." You have the power to receive whatever you ask for. If you speak positively, you will reap a good return. Watch your words!

Refocus your mind daily if this is your struggle. Focus your thoughts on your core values and the outcomes you want. Practice self-respect and self-appreciation. They will give you the optimism needed to get to fulfillment. Regularly self-reflect to maintain balance and stay focused on what matters most in your life.

---

### Moving Forward

**Self-awareness:** Monitor your social, mental, physical, and well-being meters. *Ask yourself consistently, "How do I feel about myself?"* Make a list of your old behaviors, the nonworking belief system in your life, and the new behaviors you want to acquire. Identify your self-worth and core values. Let them be your driving forces to move you toward your goals.

**Self-determination:** Avoid assigning blame to others, take ownership of your role, and stop making excuses. Know why you are engaging in any activity. Make the connections to achieve growth, knowledge, and fulfillment. You must gain autonomy over your life and take control of your choices. Do not let people's viewpoints about you or your capacity to perform interrupt your focus.

**Self-efficacy:** Believe in your strengths and abilities. Exercise control over your behavior and environment. Do not let other people's actions control your reaction or let small losses and obstacles distract you. Strive to attain high self-efficacy by being willing to get out of your comfort zone, face challenges, try new experiences, and master them.

**Self-fulfilling prophecy:** There is power in positive thinking and expectation. Be mindful of your involuntary thoughts, attitude, and communication. Your predictions and expectations affect your behavior, producing an outcome consistent with that belief. Flee from any form of self-defeating prophecy. Expect high achievement, predict success, and model goal-achieving behavior. Manifest the life you want by strategically claiming and expecting your desires to be fulfilled.

**Self-management:** To prevent your motivation from dwindling, strive for balance. Know who you are and are not. Manage your responsibilities with a plan to take on one task at a time. Be conscious of your thoughts, feelings, and actions throughout the day—practice self-care and mindfulness to keep you motivated. The act of mindfulness is being aware of your actions, environment, and what you are experiencing through your senses, thoughts, and emotions. Create space and time to pay attention to what is happening to you and in you at the present moment.

CHAPTER 11

# Principle 9
# Engage in Conscientious Relationships

*"We have a responsibility to influence the people in our lives to be the best possible people they can be: 'Therefore encourage one another and build each other up'* (1 Thessalonians 5:11)."
–Henry Cloud and John Townsend

Writing this book in weeks was a result of my established relationships. I have authors who have mentored and coached me on the best strategies to deploy if I embark on this journey. Also, I have a life partner who keeps me accountable. One Saturday morning, my husband, Tunde, said, "Kemi, you have been talking about writing a book for a while now. Why don't you start by writing your preface first?" Knowing how I like challenges, I completed it in under an hour. That was how I began writing. I went online and searched for faith-based writing clubs, and I joined two of them. They were one of the best investments I made for myself.

*Have you considered what effect your relationships have on your goals? What do relationships have to do with achieving your goals?* You must have heard of the cliché that says, "Show me your friends, and I will tell you who you are."

The people in your circle can keep you stagnant, cause you to move backward, or propel you forward in life. If you keep like-minded people in your corner, you are most likely to succeed in achieving your goals.

*How about deliberately creating the village you want?* Your village should be composed of people you contact at conferences, work, gym, church, professional organizations, school, bank, neighbors, events, and your family and friends. *So, who are the people in your network? What type of people are they? What things are these people pursuing in their lives? Do you share common goals? Or are they already where you want to be? Whom do you hang around with in your moments of glory?* Consider how your relationships have affected your goals.

Your currency is your relationship. Are you transparent enough to connect with others? Making connections often requires some level of vulnerability and trust. You will need to remove your mask and veil to cultivate meaningful relationships beyond the surface level and form deeper roots. Harness your light and speak with authenticity when you meet people. Theodore Roosevelt said, "People won't care how much you know until they know how much you care."

People often respond to you based on your energy level and presence. Lead with intentionality. When I go to conferences, I am hyper vigilant with my interactions. I study the program and attend the sessions where I want to interact with people with certain traits, attributes, or interests. Periodically, I search for events to attend based on my interests, the speakers, the program information, and the opportunity to network with people with a certain mindset.

To have a purposeful, valuable relationship, you must be of value yourself. *What value do you bring to your relationships? What are you donating to your established relationships?* Is it your time, knowledge, wisdom, or nothing? Myles Munroe eloquently said, "The value of a life is not in its duration but its donation."

So live effectively! If you want to ascend to an elevated state in life, you must learn to serve others. Serve people to help them be better than you found them and look for ways to create value in their lives. As you do so, you donate to their lives and allow your light to brighten theirs. Concentrate on being a blessing conduit and forming strong bonds. Get rid of the spirit of competition with others. Note that we are all on different journeys. However, commit to being influential and making a difference in other people's lives. Do this and watch how your life goals will transform.

> *"The power of relationship. Those who hate you do not matter, It's those who love you that count."*
> –Apostle Joshua Selman

In whatever relationship you have, be it boss and employee, parent and child, student and teacher, spousal relationship, or friendship, work on serving people better and bringing value into their lives.

One of the pieces of advice given to my husband and me as a newlywed couple that I still practice to this day is that we should both focus on serving each other's needs and watch how both of our needs get attention. When you can support others in achieving their goals, it becomes easier for the other party to support your goals and aspirations without any sense of obligation.

Another tip I practice in my relationships is to ask for assistance. I typically like things done in a particular way, which can slow down my productivity. So, I have learned to seek help from others. When you do, you are creating opportunities to gain assistance, learn to grow as an individual, and empower others. If you have a valuable relationship, you will leave footprints in people's hearts even after the relationship is over.

*What is your relationship with yourself? Are you accountable to yourself? What do you profess about yourself? How does your behavior correlate with your successes or failures? What sets of behaviors are presenting adverse outcomes in your life?* Do not let your failed history predict your future. The behavior you exhibit will determine your success, so start behaving like you are already successful so that it predicts a positive outcome.

To contribute substantially to your relationships, you must have a loving relationship with yourself. Be comfortable loving yourself and treating yourself nicely. Know and accept your strengths, weaknesses, cockiness, delights, limits, and boundaries. Have a healthy outlook on who you are. Be good to yourself and give yourself the same love you give everyone else.

Be sure to understand others' perceptions of you, but your opinion of yourself is the ultimate factor in achieving your goals. Eleanor Roosevelt eloquently stated, "No one can make you feel inferior without your consent." T. D. Jakes said, "Stop wasting your weapons on what people say about you. It is not what they say that matters. It is what I say about myself that threatens my destiny. You will never be defeated by what they say about you, but you will be defeated by what you say about yourself." Tell yourself the truth about yourself.

Discover and develop yourself. Start being passionate about who you are. We extend grace to others but not to ourselves. Have a little grace for yourself and get back on the wagon. Don't let anyone stop you from achieving your goals and dreams. Ayn Rand, the writer and philosopher, said, "The question isn't who is going to let me; it's who is going to stop me."

You do not need anyone's permission to proceed full speed ahead. Identify and uncover your purpose. What are your goals? Know and pursue them.

To know the relationships to watch out for, take assessments of everyone who walks into your life. Examine the content of your conversations. Is it about generating the next inventions, like ideas that revolutionize your environment, or is it about other people's business that does not serve anyone? When you share your goals with others, do they support you or try to shut them down? Beware of dream killers in your circle. Note that if your absence doesn't affect the people in your circle, your presence may never have mattered. Learn to set healthy boundaries and practice saying "no."

Creating new relationships takes time and effort. First, categorize your goals and align yourself with people who can help you reach them. Sometimes those people are already in your circle, so use their talents and maximize your connections. Study what others have done concerning your desired goal, and then implement their principles to achieve your goals.

One of my colleagues mentioned that he dressed like the job he wanted before getting the job, and by doing so, he picked up another attribute of his next-level desirable position.

Deliberately seek mentors who have already accomplished your goals or accountability partners who are working on similar goals. Not everyone you ask will respond favorably, so be okay with hearing "no," but do not give up on the task. When you eventually get a mentor, set up regular meetings and be intentional about your discussion. Always go prepared. Create your wish list and let them know what and how you want them to assist you. Value the time and minimize small talk. Don't be fixated on one mentor; be willing to let your mentors go and acquire new ones. Overall, position yourself for God to line up conscientious people in your path to walk with you toward your goals.

Conscientiousness is one of the five-factor personality models studied by Drs. Costa and McCrae. It can be measured by the revised NEO personality inventory (NEO PI-R) framework to predict job performance and other contextual behaviors. Conscientiousness is described in the NEO PI-R domain by six associated "facet scales": Competence, Order, Dutifulness, Achievement Striving, Self-Discipline, and Deliberation.

Eight items are used to assess each facet scale. People who scored highly on conscientiousness exhibited all six facets to a high degree. At the same time, the behavior of those with a low level of conscientiousness correlated with procrastination and low self-motivation. Also, these people are less likely to finish their desired tasks. These people are often less goal-oriented than conscientious people.

Ideally, having conscientious relationships will enhance the fulfillment of your goals. Strive to be conscientious and have relationships with others who are also conscientious. These people are efficient, highly organized, live healthily, and are generally dependable, hardworking, and persevering.

In general, highly conscientious people have self-discipline and exhibit responsible and responsive behaviors toward their spouses, and as such, they are less susceptible to getting divorced. They provide a great support system because their conscientiousness is influential and will impact their quality of life, according to a 2009 study by Brent W. Roberts and others. A higher level of conscientiousness was linked to a better quality of life. If you have these people in your life, appreciate them and share your goals with them. You will benefit from what the study termed the *"compensatory conscientiousness"* effect. As simply termed, it is the beneficial gain received because of being in a conscientious relationship to the degree that a spouse's health outcome can be predicted by their partner's conscientiousness beyond the spouse's personality.

A few years ago, after turning forty, I challenged myself to accomplish goals I should have done while I was a child. I took swimming lessons, learned how to ride a bike, and went outdoor camping. I was able to accomplish all this by working with conscientious people. When you start building intentional relationships, you might feel uncomfortable initially and find it challenging since this is something new. But don't give up. As much as you let them, highly conscientious people will do everything possible to encourage you and calm your fears. Find those people. They will provide compliments and applaud you along the way too. Learn from them, reciprocate, and ensure you move with the right intention. Forming healthy new habits can heal you.

---

**Moving Forward**

**Awareness**: Watch your associations. Identify your existing relationships. Know your doubters, encouragers, pessimists, and uplifters. Deliberately assess everyone who wants to come into your circle. In every relationship, conduct a personality assessment regularly to learn what is and is not working and adjust accordingly.

**Integrity:** Examine your core values, ethics, and moral principles. Live by them and be transparent about how you live. Be accountable and consistent, and keep your agreements in all relationships. Say what you mean, and mean what you say. Walk with people of integrity who share similar core values and morals. Integrity attracts fulfilling relationships and moves you towards accomplishing your goals.

**Conscientiousness:** Work on being a conscientious person. Select behaviors that drive success. Decide to make new choices that move you closer to being self-disciplined, organized, reliable, deliberate, and goal-seeking. Focus on networking and building relationships with conscientious people.

**Connection's intelligence:** Let your connection with others be intentional. Look for societies, local groups, organizations, and clubs in the area you want to grow in and join them. Actively participate in one or two organizations simultaneously and make a difference. Don't just sign up to be on a committee; commit to serving purposefully.

**Leave your past behind:** To move forward, you cannot keep looking backward and still make it to your destination efficiently. Your negative history doesn't have to predict your future. Learn from your past relationships. Reflect on the impact of your actions on the outcome of those relationships and your goals. How did those relationships affect your goals? Do you attract the same kind of relationships? Is there something you say or do, or the places you go, that attract people of the same character? Once you discover your contributing factor(s), leave it in the past. Note that you cannot do anything to change what happened, so don't self-loathe and let it limit or define your future. Instead, devise a new plan that propels you toward healthy and intentional relationships.

**Own your story**: Since the past is in the past, own your story—scars, and beauty marks, all the same. Appreciate them. They made you who you are today. Come to terms with your experiences. Use them to redefine and reclaim yourself. For instance, reclaim your dignity if you have lost it. Earn respect by loving yourself first and honoring yourself first. Respect others, but refuse to be disrespected. Watch your choices. Stop making permanent decisions over temporary situations; note that this shall pass.

CHAPTER 12

# Principle 10
# Communicate Your Goals

*"Ask and it will be given to you; seek and you will find;
knock and the door will be opened to you."*
(Matthew 7:7 NIV)

Countless times in my career, I have accomplished a task by merely sharing my vision with others. The Women Empowerment and Building (W.E.B.) group was established by telling friends about my dream to educate women on how to reach their full potential. Then Nancy, a friend from the group, shared a similar goal with plans already underway with an existing nonprofit organization in the community. From that one-night conversation, we developed a plan, and now the group has been going strong for many years.

According to the Bible, communication with others assists people in carrying out their God-given mission. Without Jethro, there would have been no Moses. Without Moses, there is no Joshua. Without Elijah, there is no Elisha. Without Naomi, there is no Ruth. And without Paul, there is no Timothy. These men and women had to encounter their mentors before reaching their destination. Who is your Naomi, Paul, Moses, or Elijah? Find them. They come in different colors, ages, and ethnicities. Do not underestimate the people who are already in your life.

Sometimes you won't know who these mentors are until you communicate what's on your heart. I joined a Meetup group of women where our discussion topic was *forgiveness*. In that group, I shared my desire to be a non-fiction writer, and the ladies started sharing authors in that genre. I looked up the first recommendation, contacted the author, and she responded. And that's how she's been my mentor ever since. Advantageously, she is also a faculty member. I have learned so much from her about authorship.

Communicating with others is integral to accomplishing goals. If you cultivate the skill, it will be the competence vehicle that drives your success. Think of communication as the map that will navigate you to your goal. I am not saying you need to share your goals with anyone or everyone you know. No. Be purposeful when communicating and know when to be quiet, when to speak, and what and how to speak. The primary goal of communication is to inform, engage, inquire, comprehend, collaborate, encourage, teach, and learn.

Employers have recognized that communication is one of the keys to achieving their goals, even more than technical skills in general. Communication has different dimensions. The means of communication can be nonverbal or verbal. When it is nonverbal, you speak through your body language, emotions, eye contact, gestures, energy, or written form. Verbal communication occurs by projecting audible sounds. You must be heard and understood when communicating. Make no assumptions, and don't pretend you can read minds. Ask questions to ensure you are being heard.

During my classes, mainly when I teach first-year students, I constantly pause to quiz them on what I have just shared to gauge their comprehension. Based on their responses, I may have to go through the concepts again to gain their understanding. Similarly, communicating your goals to those who can impact them ensures you gain clarity. When working on a National Science Foundation grant, I sought out people who had received the same grant for directions and best practices. The guidance I received was invaluable, including the unwritten rules.

After you have written your goals and drafted an execution plan, what should you do next? Bring your plan into submission under God's authority. Communicate what you want. Don't assume that because He is the Almighty God, He already knows what you want and what your heart desires. Yes, you are right that He understands, but He wants you to share what's on your heart with Him. He wants to commune as a Father and child do. Ask Him whatever you want, and He will meet you at the point of your needs.

You can communicate your goals through your giving. I have learned that whenever we offer a sacrificial offering to the Lord, the seed offering should be accompanied by a request or directions, like we are sending it on an errand. But if we do not do that, the offering is merely a donation. The concept of assigning your seed offering directions is like setting the keys to open doors in your life and having an avenue to tell God your desires. Communicate your goals, dreams, and aspirations to God through prayers.

Prayers catapult your needs and position them for divine intervention. Read about the experience of Paul and Silas in the jailhouse in Acts 16:25–34 (NIV). The Scripture said they prayed and sang praises to God, and "all the prison doors flew open." Note that it wasn't that some doors opened. No, all the doors flew open.

An instant release can happen when you lay your dreams before God. Paul and Silas' barrier to life was lifted, and everyone in the jailhouse had freedom because of the two men's decision. Their communication approach impacted generations. Other prisoners got released too. Speak forth your wants and needs to God in prayers and praises and watch what He will do in your life.

Learn how to call upon the Lord—not by lamenting but by singing praises. Praise to God is an instrument for your breakthroughs. It helps push you into a new season of your life. However, you need to start praising God before things go wrong and as you go through your storms. Sing praises with confidence that what you want will manifest. Praise God to bring forth your thanksgiving.

The Lord will turn around everything for your good. Your promotion to the next level is here. Go for it. Engage in meaningful praises in your private hour, where only you and your goal redeemer are present. Sing, dance, and rejoice like you already have what you want. Your devotion is how you launch into new opportunities.

When communicating with people, learn the effective keys of communication. Concerning your defined goals and objectives, examine the role of communication. Do your research. What are the gaps you want to fill through communication? Identify your primary contacts and the information needed.

Next, learn how to market yourself or your ideas if this is relevant to your goals. How can you sound convincing? What communication skills do you lack or need to sharpen? Sometimes you might be better at communicating one-on-one in conversations but not as much in large groups, so the key is to know your audience and get them engaged and interested in listening to what you have to say. With either audience, you should know upfront what your desired outcome is. Draft a plan and an agenda for your conversation. Strategize when, where, and how you will approach your topic of conversation.

In approaching a conversation, prepare to speak objectively. Objectivity shows that you are open-minded and tolerant. If you must share your point of view, be mindful to differentiate an opinion from factual information. Stay away from bias or preconceptions. Aim to speak factually to gain understanding from your participant. During the conversation, be flexible with your agenda. Based on the interaction and feedback you are getting at that moment, you might need to make quick adjustments. Be willing to move your discussion topics around or scratch them all together based on the energy you are receiving or your perceived outlook. Whether your conversation is going well or not, control your emotions, especially in a professional setting. Moderately show physical expressions of emotions, such as sadness, hurt, or excitement. Any overexpression of emotions might negatively impact the results of the conversation. Rather, verbalize a brief response like "I look forward to working with you." Show humility regardless of the hierarchy with which you are conversing. Humility and assertiveness collectively will fetch better results than arrogance.

Effective communication goes beyond what is being said or heard. Suppose you want to comprehend the information being passed across and discern the speaker's intent. In that case, you have to factor in the total body response, including your body language, such as a handshake, eye contact, tone, facial expression, and gesticulation. It would be best to consider this feedback to understand the context of what's conveyed and its implications. Learn what those responses mean. For someone like me, my facial expression at times is all you need to see to know what I think about a topic. Of course, I must consciously manage my expression in certain environments. People's body language communication should be observed and understood.

Practice active listening by measuring both verbal and nonverbal feedback responses. Being fully conscious and attentive in conversations shows meaningful engagement and establishes a better relationship. You will make a good impression and position the conversation for effective interaction if you practice active listening. Apply active listening skills by paraphrasing, summarizing, asking clarifying questions, and responding thoughtfully with supportive body cues like nodding your head or maintaining good eye contact. Refrain from interrupting the conversation, multitasking, or allowing yourself to be easily distracted by the environment.

After the communication, make sure to follow up in writing if appropriate. That's where you send a thank-you note, summarize the highlights of the topic discussed, and state the call to action and the expected date or timeline. The follow-up practice shows your level of commitment, clarifies any misunderstandings, and sets the expectation for your future interaction. Before sending a note, please use the proper salutation and a spelling and grammar checker. You do not want your message to be devalued.

Strategically identify with whom to share your goals and aspirations. Intentional communication is key to unlocking success and is paramount to your advancement and growth. It can make or break you. Through this process, accountability partners are formed.

Others can also lift you in prayer. Share your goals with people who can help you on your journey toward success. These could be people who have experience getting you where you want to go. If you have professional goals, consider talking to experts in those fields. Should it be personal goals, look for role models in your community, family, friends, or church. Also, look for an avenue to help others when they share their goals with you. Be mindful that not all goals need to be shared with everyone always. However, sharing your goals can create a productive and supportive team to cheer each other to the finish line.

**Make Declarations**

Communicate your goals to yourself and God through self-proclamations. The power of affirmations has been proven to manifest when practiced with good intentions. Affirmations are statements that, when repeated, can change your behaviors, mindset, and mood, leading to a new level of self-awareness and achieving your goals and dreams.

God is the author of declarative statements. Romans 4:17 (NKJV) says, "God, who gives life to the dead and calls those things which do not exist as though they did." All the declarations God made over Abraham came alive. Jesus also made declarations. We can account for at least seven statements He made about Himself. Everywhere Jesus went, He would declare who He was by saying:

> "I am the true vine" (John 15:1).
> "I am the way, the truth, and the life" (John 14:6).
> "I am the bread of life" (John 6:35).
> "I am the light of the world" (John 8:12).
> "I am the door of the sheep" (John 10:7).
> "I am the good shepherd" (John 10:11).
> "I am the resurrection and the life" (John 11:25).

And Jesus lived up to His statements.

*"Your brain will work tirelessly to achieve the statements you give your subconscious mind. And when those statements are the affirmations and images of your goals, you are destined to achieve them!"*

–Jack Canfield

To create your statements, you want to start with the end in mind. Know what you want to accomplish and then create your "I am" statement. For instance, if your goal is to lose weight, your statement could be, "I am ten pounds lighter than last year." If you have been bound to your past challenges and struggles and want to start living far from them, your statements could be "I am no longer bound to my past" and "I am free to receive a glorious future through Christian living." What you are doing is feeding your goals with positive statements. Plant the seed of intention by addressing what is not as if it were.

Activate your goals through biblical affirmations based on God's promises. If you need healing, declare, "I am healed through Christ that strengthens me" (Philippians 4:13). Or you could say, "I am strong" (1 Corinthians 2:10). Do you need a blessing? Say, "I am blessed with every spiritual blessing" (Ephesians 1:3). If it is forgiveness, declare, "I am forgiven" (Ephesians 1:7). Do you want to be secured? Then declare, "I am complete in God" (Colossians 2:10).

---

**Moving Forward**

**Intentions**: Clearly define the essence of your communication. Is it to gain knowledge, inquire, or inform? You want to work backward by knowing your desired outcome first, then walk through the steps needed to achieve your end goal. For instance, you want to have $5,000 in savings within a certain period, so you might ask your boss about the possible avenues to earn more income to fulfill that goal. Then proceed with the steps necessary to save a certain amount of money that would add up to your target amount within your set interval.

**Words**: Plant your words and nurture them. Words are powerful tools of communication. Our word has the power to hurt or heal. Choose them wisely. Let your words bring life to your goals, not break them. Selecting the appropriate words for engagement can transform your conversation and yield your expected outcome. Be generous with kind words while avoiding condescending or negative ones. Know how to phrase your wants or needs without sounding desperate, and learn the sequence of your communication.

**Actions**: Let your actions during and after you communicate your goals align. Proceed with the next steps by following up with a thank-you note. But most importantly, proceed with the actions suggested during the meeting. A goal without a plan equals no action.

**Body language:** Watch your nonverbal cues. Know the ones you exhibit and practice managing them while communicating your goals. Practice numerous times with friends until you have mastered how to control any negative body language.

**Prayer:** The Lord is always ready and wants to hear from you. Seek His face, and He will communicate with you. Only God can order your steps and direct your path to reach your goals. Take every single item on your goal list to Him first. Use any or all of His qualifiers in your prayers and ask for whatever you want. He is the *Goal Redeemer*!

# Acknowledgments

My gratitude goes to the *Next STEPP Center*, St. Petersburg, FL, Women Empowerment and Building (W.E.B.) members, and my co-facilitator for giving me an audience and support to craft the chapters of this book. Thank you to the Goal Redeemers Connect Group at the *Citylife Church*, Tampa, FL, for your tremendous support in piloting the book as a course. To *Akron Summit Scribes, LLC* and the *Straight from His Plate-Christian* writers' groups for your writer's coaching platform and space to launch the hidden words on paper. I would be remiss if I did not acknowledge the *Word of Faith Covenant Ministries, Chapel of Faith*, Tampa, FL, for their drive to make me a vessel and for encouraging me to preach some of the book chapters when I wanted to remain silent.

To my development editor, Barbados Kios, who was the first to read the manuscript, thank you for your guidance and enlightenment. To Ellena Balkcom, founder of *Written on Purpose Communications*, for providing the copy editing. And to Tiana Joe for line editing and to Abbey McLaughlin for your proofreading service. To all my book endorsers, Pastor Lisa Singh of *Heavenly Grace Ministries*, New York, thank you for honoring my invitation to review this book. Your written foreword is a book within a book. To Sandra Heard, President of *Heard Empowerment, LLC*, my writing coach and divine God connection, your inspiration, authenticity, and call to dig deeper are second to none. To Nancy Lewis, my friend, and W.E.B. co-host and facilitator, thank you for being my co-creator and striving to stay true to the call. To Apostle Ada Davis of *Jesus Church Ministries of Tampa*, for your prayers and accountability throughout the writing phase. To Mercy Adebayo, my friend, thank you for always being transparent and demonstrating the life of a disciple. To my Beta Readers, Cynthia Head and Delon Turpin, I thank you for your feedback and constructive criticism.

Thanks to my family, the Akintewe, Ayodeji, and Akinje, for your love and support. To my children, Toye and Teni, for inspiring the book cover design. And to my beloved husband, Tunde, for challenging me to start writing.

Utmostly, I acknowledge the Holy Spirit for His guidance in writing this book. I am forever grateful to my Goal Redeemer, the Lord Jesus Christ, for His faithfulness and grace enabled me to accomplish my goals.

# About the Author

Dr. Kemi Akintewe was born in Washington, D.C., and raised in Nigeria, West Africa. By seventeen, she moved to New York City and designed her roadmap to success, entailing what she wanted to accomplish in life. Today, she is an engineering professor at a higher education institution, a wife, and a mother of two children. She is an inspirationalist, a certified success coach, and a conscientious mentor who believes everyone can reach their full potential by positioning themselves for God to do His work. She has written her debut book titled *Goal Redeemer: 10 Principles for Overcoming Barriers to Achieving Your Goals and Fulfilling Your God-Given Dreams* to inspire others to accomplish their goals despite self-inflicting obstacles.

# ABOUT THE AUTHOR

The author describes herself as a lifelong learner of personal development. Her passion for spiritual growth drives her success. Dr. Akintewe adheres to the principles of having a growth mindset, which does not see failures as setbacks but as opportunities to consider other approaches to fulfilling the ascribed goals. She hosts and facilitates women's empowerment sessions and goal-setting workshops across various institutions.

She can be reached at Info@DrKemiAkintewe.com or www.DrKemiAkintewe.com

# Bibliography

American Association for the Advancement of Science (AAAS) "Science Careers myIDP Individual Development Plan" accessed September 8, 2022, http://myidp.sciencecareers.org/.

Bandura, A. Self-efficacy: *Toward a unifying theory of behavioral change.* Psychological Review, 84(2), 191-215, 1977.

Costa, Paul and McCrae, Robert R. *The Five-Factor Model, Five-Factor Theory, and Interpersonal Psychology.* National Institute on Aging, NIH, DHHS, 2012.

Covey, Stephen R.; Merrill, A. Roger; Merrill, Rebecca R. *First Things First: To Live, to Love, to Learn, to Leave a Legacy.* New York: Simon & Schuster, 1994.

Doran, George; Miller, Arthur; Cunningham, James. "*There's a S.M.A.R.T. way to write management goals and objectives.*" Management Review, Vol. 70, Issue 11, 35-36, 1981.

Dyer, Wayne. "How To Forgive Someone Who Has Hurt You: In 15 Steps." Even When Forgiveness Feels Impossible (blog). Dr. Wayne W. Dyer. June 18, 2015. https://www.drwaynedyer.com/blog/how-to-forgive-someone- in-15-steps/.

Enright, R. D. *Forgiveness Is a Choice: A Step-by-Step Process for Resolving Anger and Restoring Hope.* Washington, DC: American Psychological Association, 2001.

Humphrey, A. *SWOT Analysis for Management Consulting.* SRI Alumni Newsletter. SRI International, 2005.

McCrae, R. R.; Costa, P. T. Jr.; Del Pilar, G. H.; Rolland, J. P.; Parker, W. D. "*Cross-cultural assessment of the five-factor model: The revised

NEO Personality Inventory". *Journal of Cross-Cultural Psychology.* 29: 171–188, 1998.

Maddux, James E., ed. *Self-efficacy, adaptation, and adjustment: Theory, research, and application.* Springer Science & Business Media, 2013.

Matthews, Gail. "The Impact of Commitment, Accountability, and Written Goals on Goal Achievement." Psychology, Faculty Presentations, 87th Convention of the Western Psychological Association, 3, 2007, https://scholar.dominican.edu/psychology-faculty-conference-presentations/3.

Maslow, A. H. *A theory of human motivation.* Psychological Review, 50(4), 370–396, 1943 https://doi.org/10.1037/h0054346.

Oettingen, Gabriele; Mayer, Doris; Sevincer, A. Timur; Stephens, Elizabeth J.; Pak, Hyeon-ju; and Hagenah, Meike. "*Mental Contrasting and Goal Commitment: The Mediating Role of Energization.*" Personality and Social Psychology Bulletin 35, no. 5: 608–22, May 2009.

Ryan RM, Deci EL. *Self-determination theory and the facilitation of intrinsic motivation, social development, and well-being.* Am Psychol. Jan;55(1):68-78, 2000.

Reiss, Steven, *Who Am I: The 16 Basic Desires That Motivate Our Behavior and Define Our Personalities* New York: Penguin Publishing Group, 2000.

Roberts BW; Smith J; Jackson JJ; Edmonds G. *Compensatory Conscientiousness and Health in Older Couples.* Psychological Science. 20(5):553- 559, 2009.

Sarah A. Schnitker, *An examination of patience and well-being,* The Journal of Positive Psychology, 7:4, 263-280, 2012. DOI: 10.1080/17439760.2012.697185.

Tracy, Brian, *Eat That Frog!: 21 Great Ways to Stop Procrastinating and Get More Done in Less Time.* San Francisco, CA: Berrett-Koehler Publishers, 2007.

Tripp, Paul. *What Did You Expect? Redeeming the Realities of Marriage.* Wheaton, Illinois: Crossway Books, 2010.

www.ingramcontent.com/pod-product-compliance
Lightning Source LLC
Chambersburg PA
CBHW030331010526
44119CB00036B/456/J